Research in Archives

ARTHUR MANN
Advisory Editor
for
American History

PHILIP C. BROOKS

Research in Archives

The Use of Unpublished Primary Sources

THE UNIVERSITY OF CHICAGO PRESS
Chicago and London

Library of Congress Catalog Card Number: 69-19273

The University of Chicago Press, Chicago 60637
The University of Chicago Press, Ltd., London W.C. 1

To Dorothy Holland Brooks

Contents

Preface

Early in my experience as an archivist and historian I felt the need for a manual for users of archives and private papers. Dr. Ernst Posner, the distinguished archivist and professor emeritus at the American University, has urged that such a manual be written, citing the example of Max Bär's *Leitfaden für Archivbenutzer* (Leipzig, 1896). That handbook contained valuable suggestions about the user's approach to archives, but much of it consisted of descriptions of major repositories, not now needed because of the extensive publication of finding aids.

A report of a survey made for the National Historical Publications Commission in 1966 noted that graduate students were not being adequately taught in the use of unpublished source materials. Among scholars there is a difference of opinion on whether the professors or the archivists should do that teaching. My own view is that the professors should do more than they usually do, while—at the same time—the staffs of repositories should be expected to explain the use of their own holdings. Wherever the teaching is done, I trust that this manual will be helpful. Almost all the numerous existing texts on historical method dwell on the use of printed materials but pass lightly over archives and private papers. This manual is intended to fill that gap—to fill it for the researcher rather than for the caretaker of materials. And, though archivists see many older researchers who do not know how to use historical materials, this manual is intended primarily for the young scholar. Although its examples are in American history, it should be useful in other fields as well.

History, it has been said, does not repeat itself—but historians often repeat each other. This manual is written, then, for those who know they must first identify the past before they can narrate or judge it. For even when working with a hypothesis, a researcher with scholarly integrity must view all the sources of information he can, and be guided by them.

The question of which sources contain the information a researcher seeks is more important than definitions of various kinds of materials, but he does need to understand the basis of such definitions. Accordingly, I have sought to deal with such problems, but in the order in which the user encounters them, rather than in the sequence of archival operations. (Methods of caring for different classes of materials are not dealt with here, although there is an emphasis on reasons why the researcher should understand the archivist's problems and policies.)

Although this manual is designed to help the user in any repository, large or small, the National Archives and Records Service and the Library of Congress receive special mention because of their size and their central character; many other extremely important institutions are cited only as they illustrate certain activities. Except for the most general, particular collections and specific finding aids are not mentioned. This is not a bibliographical work, and it is not meant to duplicate the *Guide to Archives and Manuscripts in the United States,* by Philip M. Hamer, or the *National Union Catalog of Manuscript Collections* being issued by the Library of Congress.

The experience upon which this book is based has been largely in a number of positions in the National Archives and Records Service through more than thirty years, and active membership in the Society of American Archivists for almost as long. The views expressed, of course, are my own and do not necessarily present the policy of either of those organizations.

Thanks are not adequate to express my gratitude to the many persons who have enabled me to complete this task. In addition to giving me his encouragement, Dr. Posner has read and commented upon much of the manuscript. Lester J. Cappon, Richard S. Kirkendall, Donald R. McCoy, Gerald T. White, and my wife have read all of it; Everett O. Alldredge, Frank G. Burke, Elizabeth B. Drewry, David C. Eberhart, Milton O. Gustafson, Oliver W. Holmes, James B. Rhoads, and Richard T. Ruetten have given valuable assistance on certain passages. The bibliographical assistance of Frank B. Evans has been helpful. Countless researchers and archivists have helped me to understand the close bond between them, and several members of the staff of the Harry S. Truman Library have assisted me in finding reference materials.

1

Archives and Private Papers

There is a fascination about handwritten papers from other days, a feeling of genuineness, a personal touch about them that brings one close to the people who produced them. This sense of reality is more than a superficial impression. On it rests the faith that historians have in "original" source materials, and it is basic to a great part of the serious research involving the past. In varying degree, it extends to kinds of materials other than handwritten that grow from human activity. Whenever we can hold anything that was actually used or produced by someone from a previous era, this sense of identification may exist. But no other type of materials tells us as much about the past as the documents in which the actors of an earlier era recorded their doings, their thoughts, their actions, and their reactions.

The riches that lie in countless repositories can be mined productively only if the seeker knows what he is looking for, where he may expect to find it, and how to recognize it. Dr. Samuel Johnson paraphrased an old Spanish proverb when he said, "He who would bring home the wealth of the Indies must carry the wealth of the Indies with him. So it is in travelling, a man must carry knowledge with him if he would bring home knowledge." We may say the same of research; a man must carry knowledge with him if he would bring home knowledge. To use unpublished sources fruitfully, the investigator, be he professional scholar or casual inquirer, should know their nature and background, their physical characteristics, and the problems that they present. He must be able to find and to select wisely those items that serve his purpose.

1

The Past and Historical Evidence

The study of the past is the study of events that took place, what people said or wrote then, and the trends that developed. Such matters cannot be changed, but the evidence of them varies widely, and their description and interpretation are often revised. The closer the student can get to direct observance of them, the closer he can come to being a witness himself, the more accurately he can narrate or understand them. With intelligent imagination he may visualize events, or sense their reality.

The quantity of documents on paper, written or graphic, in comparison with other kinds of "documents" such as artifacts and monuments included in the broader sense of that word, is of course greater for recent periods of history than for those long past. The historical student always hopes to find those documents that were created in connection with the events he is studying, just as they were at that time, without marking, rearrangement, damage, or other change that would mar their purity as evidence.

The forms in which historical evidence does exist, however, lead us to certain problems of definitions. For some of the characteristics that cause various kinds of materials to be called by different names derive from the manner in which they have been preserved rather than from their original nature. These definitions should be understood by the researcher so that he can appreciate what he is using, and can state his needs to the archivist.

Unpublished Primary Sources

"Original," "source," and "primary" all have the connotation of being firsthand. "Source" is the most general term and may apply to anything from which we derive information. It is often used in research as referring to the initial or ultimate source, something analogous to the source of a river, but its definition does not limit it to that sense. "Original" not only has many other connotations, but even within the field of research may have several meanings. Neither of these terms carries a sufficiently definite idea to be useful alone. "Primary," as distinguished from "secondary," does imply a direct derivation from the persons or events one is studying.

Thus in this manual the general class of items which are being discussed will be referred to as unpublished primary sources—they are the raw materials for study.[1]

Primary sources, in our sense, may have been preserved intentionally by an organization, be it governmental, business, religious, institutional, or even a private family, as evidence of its own activity for its own future use or to tell its story to posterity. Such primary sources may have come into the hands of an agency whose major task is the preservation of source materials perhaps of many different origins for the use of persons who wish to consult them, or they may have been gathered by persons who have an interest in possessing things of a historical nature.

Our materials will generally be referred to as "unpublished," rather than "unprinted," because the latter term hardly serves to make the necessary distinction. Archives often include some printed items, but the published editions of documents are not within the main focus of this manual.

The Archivist

Unpublished primary source materials have been handled through the years in many different ways and by widely varying types of persons. Work with them is often difficult and tedious, and frequently their care is a labor of love by individuals who like to work with the "stuff of history." Official archivists, custodians of private papers, writers seeking grist for their own mills, those who enjoy or make a business of collecting and buying or selling rare items, and many others

1. Jacques Barzun and Henry F. Graff, *The Modern Researcher* (New York: Harcourt, Brace & Co., 1957), p. 98.

have shared in this work. One result is that confusion has de-veloped over the terms that should be used to describe the materials and the ways in which they are handled. Additionally, usages change from one period to another. Finally, those who care for the sources are often too close to them to see their own broad common interest. Despite this confusion, of course, the researcher's interest should always be focused on the informational value of his sources, not on the sometimes unfortunate usage differences among their caretakers.

Though the user should not have to become embroiled in terminological disputes, he is likely to hear or read of them as he associates with those who care for historical sources. Thus he needs some broad understanding of the major categories of materials in order to explain his needs and to understand the descriptions of sources that he might use. In this manual, then, the terms "archives" and "private papers" will be used as circumstances warrant to cover all unpublished primary sources; the persons who deal with them will be referred to as "archivists." It would otherwise require involved circumlocutions and the use of quite ambiguous words to deal with all the possible variations of origin, ownership, and responsibility for the care of unpublished primary source materials.

This usage follows the precedent of the Ad Hoc Committee on Historical Manuscripts of the American Historical Association in its significant report of 1950.[2] It also follows the intent of the framers of the Society of American Archivists (which was established in 1936). It is not intended to express any difference in comparative importance, nor to suggest changes in the usages of existing institutions, but rather to emphasize their common concerns. All those responsible for unpublished primary sources must bring them together, provide for their physical preservation, arrange and describe them for prospective users, and should provide reference service on them. The fact that these responsibilities are common to all is a strong argument for the user of a common term for which "archivist"

2. *Proceedings of the American Historical Association, 1950* (Washington: Government Printing Office, 1951), pp. 64–71.

is the most suitable. (The word "custodian" seems hardly adequate as a common denominator since it does not convey the proper connotation of intellectual control of one's holdings. The term "curator" will not stand without involved modification since it is used for persons in charge of many other types of materials, such as art treasures and museum objects. The British title of "keeper," used for the principal official in charge of the nation's records, is not used in the same sense in the United States. In the Library of Congress, for example, "keeper" was once used to refer to the person charged with the difficult technical responsibility of physical protection of all kinds of collections, but it has been dropped.)

Archives and Private Papers

The principal difficulty, if one goes further into distinctions, lies between usages of the words "manuscripts" and "archives." This difficulty has developed largely from the diversity of practices in the United States, which has not had the binding factor of tradition that has existed in Europe. Dr. Ernst Posner, when he was president of the Society of American Archivists, once remarked that

> the American archivist has found himself confronted with what seems to me to be an unfortunate dichotomy, that between archives and historical manuscripts, unknown in the countries of the European continent. Influenced by the English concept of the "public record" as the legal record, a concept that only slowly gave way to a broader interpretation embracing the papers of administrative departments, we reduced the archives of informal organizations, families, and individuals to the level of historical manuscripts, subjected them to methods not compatible with their very nature, and erected an artificial gulf between archivists and manuscript custodians.[3]

3. Ernst Posner, "What, Then, Is the American Archivist, This New Man?" *American Archivist,* 20 (1957): p. 7.

Just as very few repositories have only one kind of material in their care, so no single person is likely to be concerned exclusively with the care of any one kind.

The respected word "manuscripts" is in one sense too broad and in another too limited for use here. We could not say that any item meeting the literal definition (that is, any item written by hand) is a primary source for historical research—there are just too many kinds of manuscripts. We find that among research materials there are typed papers, maps and charts, photographs, and other physical types of items that are not manuscripts in the strictest sense but that *are* important primary sources.

The word "manuscript" is, of course, used in the title of one of the greatest concentrations of primary source materials to which the scholar can turn, the Manuscript Division of the Library of Congress. It is important to note, however, that the Manuscript Division houses all kinds of manuscripts, including those that we think of as "literary" as well as those we think of as primarily "historical," and that one could not easily make a clear distinction between the two. The Manuscript Society also uses the term in a broad sense in describing itself as "an international society of autograph collectors established to foster the greater use of original source manuscript material in the study, teaching, and writing of history. . . ."[4]

The modification of the term "manuscripts" by the addition of the word "historical"—perhaps originally to distinguish them from literary manuscripts—is widely used, though it has resulted in much confusion. Its broad scope, including both organized and unorganized papers, is best set forth in Dr. Lester J. Cappon's statement that the term

> historical manuscripts may cover (1) bodies or groups of papers with organic unity, in the nature of archives, personal or institutional; (2) artificial collections of manuscripts acquired by a private collector from various

4. Statement published in each issue of *Manuscripts* magazine; for example, vol. 20, no. 3 (Summer, 1968), back cover.

sources, usually according to plan but without regard for *respect des fonds*; (3) individual manuscripts acquired by the repository for their special importance to research and comprising a collection of what, for want of a better term, are sometimes called "miscellaneous manuscripts."[5]

One is tempted to paraphrase a quotation from Horace Greeley, who is alleged to have said that while all Democrats were not horse thieves, all horse thieves were Democrats. We might say that while all historical manuscripts are not archives, all archives are historical manuscripts. But even that would not hold, for we have the maps, photographs, and other physical types that are not strictly manuscripts.

Dr. Posner, after quoting the Cappon definition, said:

> For unorganized papers of a personal nature the term historical manuscripts is now being superseded by the term "private papers." For "bodies or groups of papers with organic unity" the term "archives" is preferred.[6]

This is the usage of this manual as well.

The Nature of Archives

The establishment of the National Archives in 1934 led people in this country to be conscious of the word "archives," a word with which most of them had not really been familiar before, though it had a long and distinguished history in some states and abroad. (One story current at that time had a waiter at a cocktail party in Washington confusing "archives" and "anchovies.")

Partly because of the fact that the largest institution of its kind is the repository for federal government records, emphasis has been put upon the term in connection with the official,

5. Lester J. Cappon, "Historical Manuscripts as Archives: Some Definitions and Their Application," *American Archivist,* 19 (1956): 104–5.
6. Ernst Posner, *American State Archives* (Chicago: University of Chicago Press, 1964), pp. 369–70.

organized records of a governmental body. This focus was strengthened by the British concept that such records lost their archival character if their lineage of custody was broken, and by uncertainty about the difficult question of just what constitute the "public records."[7]

Recent usage is that of the more comprehensive definition in Dr. Posner's book on state archives, which describes archives as

> records of a government agency or other organization or institution having enduring values because of the information they contain. The term is also applied to the records of families and individuals, especially if consciously organized for preservation.[8]

Official Records and Personal Papers

An important point to note is that while an item among the records of an organization and another discrete item in a collection of private papers may look quite alike, their significance as historical evidence may be very different. Their relationship to other materials is important. Official records have grown as bodies of material, often referred to as "files," representing the lives of organizations and preserved according to their functions and development. Private papers may be as carefully preserved from their origin, or from their arrival in a repository, but without arrangement derived from their initial use they cannot tell the historian as much about the persons or events that they represent.

The researcher should recognize that hardly any substantial topic can be studied on the basis of one kind of materials alone. The official records of an organization, for example, may provide the framework, the skeleton, of a historical nar-

7. For a scholarly study of this problem, see Oliver W. Holmes, " 'Public Records'—Who Knows What They Are?" *American Archivist,* 23 (1960): 3–26.

8. Posner, *American State Archives,* p. 368.

rative. Private correspondence or memoirs can enrich it with the flesh of personal feeling, opinion, or interpretation.

This suggests another basis of distinction, which often corresponds to the sometimes vague line between organizational records and private papers: that is the difference between the more formal records that one creates as a member of an organization, including correspondence, and the letters, memoirs, diaries, and the like that he writes as a private individual. These are sometimes classified as "official" and "personal" materials, a distinction which is especially important when we consider legal problems.

The answer to no question is more elusive to historians than *why* people acted or thought as they did—and the answer is likely to be found in diverse sources. While the official documentation of an event may tell what happened, and may give a formal reason or justification, the human story of how the thoughts and wishes of individuals brought forth certain actions may have been told in more personal, less formal writings.

An example of the vividness of this kind of informal writing (albeit one of a quality not often found) is seen in John Quincy Adams' diary note of the signing of the Treaty of 1819 with Spain (by himself and Luis de Onís, the Spanish minister). Of this agreement, which provided for the cession of the Floridas and the recognition of the United States claim to land westward to the Pacific, Adams wrote:

> It was, perhaps, the most important day of my life. . . . The acquisition of the Floridas has long been an object of earnest desire to this country. The acknowledgment of a definite line of boundary to the South Sea forms a great epocha in our history. The first proposal of it in this negotiation was my own, and I trust it is now secured beyond the reach of revocation.[9]

Later Adams learned that a confusion regarding certain grants of lands to Spaniards that he thought had been nullified

9. John Quincy Adams, *Memoirs* . . . (Philadelphia: J. B. Lippincott, 1874–77), 4: 274–75.

threatened the ratification of the treaty. When it was finally accomplished, he wrote in language that one would hardly find in official correspondence:

> Under the petals of this garland of roses the Scapin, Onís, had hidden a viper. His mock sickness . . . his fraudulent declarations to me, and his shuffling equivocations here and in Spain, to acquire the reputation of having duped the President and me, were but materials in the hands of my enemies to dose me with the poison extracted from the laurels of the treaty itself.[10]

Published Sources

The example from Adams' diary illustrates another point, regarding unpublished sources, for his diary is available to students both in print and on microfilm (issued by the Massachusetts Historical Society). Many bodies of documents are, indeed, reproduced for dissemination among libraries and readers. Outstanding examples are the several series of letterpress publications sponsored by the National Historical Publications Commission; the *Territorial Papers of the United States* formerly published by the Department of State and more recently by the National Archives and Records Service; the *Foreign Relations* series of the Department of State; and the National Archives' Microfilm Publication series. Such issuances exemplify the skill and judgment of historical and editorial scholars, and are widely used in research. The editors have solved many of the problems of criticism of the texts that would otherwise face the scholars.

But only an extremely small and select portion of the total volume of primary source materials can be published in print or on film. The researcher must still go to unpublished materials for most of his information. Thus he must find them, understand their characteristics, and be able to mine them productively.

10. *Ibid,* 5: 290.

Characteristics of Unpublished Sources

Several characteristics are common to all kinds of unpublished primary sources. Uniqueness is the most significant. Practically by definition they are not duplicated. Although in recent decades the means of making multiple copies of documents have grown rapidly, different copies are likely to have slightly different forms, to have additions or notations subsequent to their creation that reflect later stages in their handling, or even to be filed with other materials in such a way that their content or their meaning for the researcher are not quite the same. One must find the key copy for his purpose, the "original" if any can be identified as such, and must understand the circumstances that produced the form in which he sees it.

Each written document may be presumed to have been created for a purpose—to effect a transaction, to convey information, or to set down a record for the future. This purpose usually has a bearing on its meaning to the research user. The extent of formality; the completeness of information; the degree to which the document was created to effect a current action; or the possibility that something was written to describe an event or a thought for posterity are all elements that should be understood. An application for a position made by a person of interest, for example, may have both transitory and lasting meaning. It is written for an immediate purpose; yet may give valuable biographical information about the person. The way he writes it to accomplish his immediate aim may affect its credibility as evidence in the long run. These are matters of historical criticism that are not really included in the subject matter of this manual, but they do have a definite relationship to the archival character of the sources.

Closely related to the purpose is the person or organization represented by an item. A document may have widely varying meanings depending upon its character. It may be a record of a government, the product of a church committee, or a personal letter of an individual, and it cannot be understood without knowing something of that government, committee, or person. Thus, while the objective of the researcher may be to produce a history of a government, or an institution, or a biography, the more background information he has about his subject from books, personal accounts, or wherever, the better use he can make of the documents. Thus, archivists stress the importance of the administrative history of governmental units—he who would bring home knowledge must carry knowledge with him.

Another characteristic that should be noted by the researcher is the location of a document in a file or a collection of related items. This may indicate that the item at hand cannot be understood without others representing the same series of actions, or simply that the person who brought discrete items together had a significant interest in their subject matter.

An Example: Mr. Ascot

The relationships of organizational records and private papers may be visualized by considering the fate of a simple letter. Suppose that a prominent alumnus of Westernland University, Mr. Ascot, writes to the president of that institution offering a gift of money to establish a fellowship fund. Being a businessman, he makes a carbon copy for his own file. It may eventually be seen there by a student working either on a biography of Mr. Ascot or a history of his company.

The original letter, signed and delivered, will be considered more authentic. It may be found among the archives of the university, in the files either of the president's office or of the fellowship committee—or the president may have valued the autograph because of the importance of Mr. Ascot, and may have kept the original among his own papers. In this day of multiple carbons and quick-copy machines, copies are probably made for Mr. Ascot's lawyers and for various university officials. Some of them may be typed rather than facsimile copies, and may be slightly inaccurate. Annotations or comments may have been written on the letter and the copies by various people. In fact, identical copies of unprinted documents seldom exist.

Filing practices may also affect the researcher's task in finding papers and his ability to see their place in the procedures that he is studying. Mr. Ascot's letter, for example, may be filed alphabetically by the writer's name, or by the subject with which it deals—a seemingly simple difference but one which will determine its place among related papers. A number of letters from Mr. Ascot filed together may tell much about him and his relations to Westernland University. On the other hand, a number of papers filed under the subject of the fellowship foundation will be valuable for study of the educational development of the institution. There are also likely, of course, to be other firsthand accounts of this fellowship offer.

Most of the subjects that researchers are likely to deal with involve more complex negotiations than this example. Matters of public affairs, governmental operations, or the activities of any large organization require the study of the doings of many people, usually in several different repositories. The pertinence of the example here is to emphasize the interrelationships of various kinds of primary sources, the difficulty of making mutually exclusive distinctions, and the necessity of using different types of materials as one's needs for information guide him.

2

Finding the Sources

The scholar's quest for the information he needs can be easy or difficult, effective or not, depending largely on his knowledge of his own requirements, his resourcefulness, the availability of finding aids, and the degree of cooperation between himself and the archivist. His success in approaching the sources can be greatly enhanced if he knows what he is after, and that in turn depends upon his having a well-defined and feasible topic of study.

Choosing a Feasible Topic

The choice of a topic, particularly for the graduate student undertaking a thesis or dissertation, is a serious matter. A project upon which the researcher is to spend months or years of his time should be chosen so that the work is feasible and the product satisfying. Available primary sources are one of the most significant factors to be considered in making this choice. Books on historiography advise care in this matter. One cautions that

> it would be an obvious error to select a subject upon which the testimony could be expected to be in a language that the investigator did not know . . . [or] if the testimony were available only in an area that would be difficult of access, or could be presumed to have disappeared, or might be costly to acquire, or belonged to private individuals who were jealous of it, or was among the restricted documents in governmental archives.

It also notes that "some wit has differentiated historical research from plagiarism by defining research as copying from more than one book, but . . . the essential difference lies in looking for some new or unused sources of information upon a subject or some new interpretation of it, or both."[1] Another author advises that the undertaking must be feasible in terms of "availability of sources to which you can have access without unreasonable inconvenience and with the assurance that you will be able to use them without the owner or the repository attempting to censor your conclusions."[2]

These quotations anticipate some of the problems which will be dealt with later, but in regard to the existence of available sources they suggest the proverbial dilemma of the chicken and the egg. One should not attempt study without the availability of sources, but one cannot determine that without preliminary study. Thus, thought, inquiry, and tentative searching are essential.

Study the Printed Material First

Writings on historical method stress the need for a careful plan of study and suggest various steps to be taken in preparation. Among these are the assembly of a tentative bibliography, preliminary reading, and a list of pertinent points to be studied. All should be done before approaching the unpublished primary sources, and the most important is the review of printed items. Rarely can even a competent researcher go directly to a body of archives and do profitable research without wasting time, duplicating someone else's work, failing to use pertinent sources, or misinterpreting those that he does see. The suggestions that follow pertain especially to those printed works that lead to primary sources, aside from the general value of background reading. They apply to a person who already has a topic, or needs specific information for some other purpose, as well as to the graduate student choosing a subject.

1. Louis Gottschalk, *Understanding History: A Primer of Historical Method* (New York: Alfred A. Knopf, 1960), pp. 66–67.
2. Wood Gray *et al.*, *Historian's Handbook: A Key to the Study and Writing of History,* 2d ed. (Boston: Houghton Mifflin Co., 1964), p. 10.

It is natural in any study plan to consult the most general printed works first, and sometimes they may provide all the information needed. Archivists are often disturbed by having inquirers "discover" in the archives data that are easily available, for example, in an encyclopedia. They are sometimes struck by the inefficiency of a student who tries to work out his initial outline from the records when this could more easily be done from reference works, general treatises, or monographs.

In order to perceive what kinds of unpublished sources he should look for, the researcher should know as much as possible about the lives of the persons whose actions he will be studying, or the administrative history of the organizations involved. For individuals, there are countless printed items, including biographical directories such as *Who's Who in America* and more extensive works such as the *Dictionary of American Biography* or published biographies. Even the traditional county or family histories, the publication of which were financed by individuals purchasing sets of books, may be useful, though they should be used with caution.

For organizations, there are handbooks such as the *Federal Government Manual* or the "blue books" issued by state governments, and historical publications of governments at the various levels, as well as specialized works. The issuance of business histories has grown rapidly in recent decades, and many universities, churches, labor unions, and other organizations have published historical and informational writings. For the assiduous student, there is no dearth of general printed material, based upon and referring to unpublished sources.

Printed works of other researchers are among the best guides to primary sources. They may directly mention or cite bodies of material, or by their discussion they may indicate what one would expect to find. A biography may refer to unpublished memoirs, for example, or may mention other persons whose papers the researcher might seek, or related places and events that would suggest the existence of files.

Footnotes and bibliographies are put in books and articles

not only to authenticate the authors' statements but to guide other inquirers to pertinent materials. Using another writer's references without actually consulting the sources he has cited may, of course, constitute plagiarism or slipshod scholarship, but historical scholars generally cooperate in developing knowledge of the past, and no one can expect to investigate every aspect of a subject. Therefore, one writer's footnotes may properly be taken as guides by other scholars as to where they may find data on the same or related subjects. Failing to use them would be sheer waste of resources.

"The learning of one man," said the noted explorer John Wesley Powell, "does not subtract from the learning of another, as if there were a limited quantity to be divided into exclusive holdings. . . . It may be wrong to take another man's purse, but it is always right to take another man's knowledge, and it is the highest virtue to promote another man's investigation."[3]

Consultation of printed books and articles is the best way to learn what aspects of historical development need further study. Perhaps there is a good story yet to be told; current events are constantly passing into historical perspective; a more incisive search of the past may lead to better understanding; or new sources on old subjects have turned up. New research techniques may make new viewpoints possible. An author may consciously suggest the need for further research, or by his omissions or his incitements to imagination may indirectly suggest the need for further work.

It may be argued that students of very recent periods find few scholarly books or articles about their subjects; this is one of the challenges facing those who delve into "contemporary" history. Yet the biblical admonition, "Of the making of many books there is no end," seems to grow ever more true. For every person, development, or event there are likely to be some printed materials that lead to unpublished sources. Indeed, some

3. Quoted in Wallace Stegner, *Beyond the Hundredth Meridian: John Wesley Powell and the Second Opening of the West* (Boston: Houghton Mifflin Co., 1954), p. 292.

phases of recent history have been treated by writings specifically designed to point out topics that warrant study and unused sources that offer opportunities.[4]

An important class of printed items to be consulted are the publications of primary sources that have been considered important enough to warrant being printed in full. They are in most cases selected from larger bodies of unprinted materials and carry editorial explanations that tell a great deal about the sources and the repositories. Many of the best series of publications in recent years have been those sponsored by the National Historical Publications Commission. In many cases, the scholar can count on the editor to produce valid texts.[5] Even so, the researcher is likely to want information about the person or organization that produced the documents, and to refer to items other than those chosen for publication. The more thorough the editing, however, the more likely is this information to be found.

This emphasis upon the use of printed materials places a high premium on the cooperation of librarians, professionals who are concerned primarily with the handling of books. They have a close affinity with archivists, but the kinds of materials the two deal with require different techniques. The student is likely to consult the librarian first, and of course can learn much from him. Specialized reference librarians often know much about subject fields and can guide the student to the most valuable materials. Research libraries, too, have many of

4. The paper, "Fields for Research in the Diplomatic History of the United States to 1900," by Samuel F. Bemis, *American Historical Review,* 36 (October, 1930): 68–75, stimulated considerable research. The sponsors of *The Truman Period as a Research Field,* ed. Richard S. Kirkendall (Columbia, Mo.: University of Missouri Press, 1967), hope the same will prove true for it.

5. Examples of scholarly editing are the papers of the Adams family being published by the Massachusetts Historical Society, and those of Thomas Jefferson and Woodrow Wilson at Princeton; the *Territorial Papers of the United States,* long published by the Department of State but now by the National Archives; and the *Papers of the Presidents of the United States,* from Truman on, being published by the Federal Register Division of the National Archives.

the printed guides that tell the nature and whereabouts of archives and private papers.

The dependence of the scholar on printed materials by no means ends when he has turned to the unpublished sources. Frequent reference to books is, of course, necessary. The researcher is fortunate when he finds a good working collection of published materials in the repository that holds the archives and private papers, since working in the papers without books at hand is akin to working in a vacuum.

Identification of Needs

As his reading progresses, the researcher will naturally build up a tentative outline, indicating what he plans to write about in his report, article, thesis, or book. Listing the additional kinds of information he needs may be like reviewing the existing clues in a detective story and considering what evidence is still needed. Just as the detective does not want to waste his time and effort on fruitless "leads," so the researcher will not want to squander his search in aimless queries. Thus the best result that can come of this planning is a listing of names of persons, places, organizations, events, questions, and problems. Such names should be entered on cards for sorting, as they will lead to different bodies of sources in various repositories. Armed with his cards, the researcher can use wisely the guides to sources, and once he has decided which to consult, can tell the archivist what he is seeking.

Resourcefulness and imagination are essential in the preliminary exploration as well as in the later actual study. One can suppose that certain kinds of sources would exist if he thinks carefully about his subject, the persons involved, the government or institutions concerned, and the kinds of records that would naturally grow out of the events that he will be studying. He should ask himself who would have produced the useful documents in the transaction he is concerned with. What would be the expected flow of events? What kinds of records would have been created? What would be the life history of the documents, from their creation through current use, filing, temporary storage, and eventual retention in a repository where he can consult them? What kinds of materials would one expect to be kept rather than discarded? These are the kinds of questions that archivists deal with, but the researcher can visualize many of the answers. The more he understands of the ways in which archivists work with these questions the more intelligent will his research be.

The researcher who knows what he wants, and is well versed from preliminary reading in the historical background of his subject, is ready to find and to use the unpublished primary sources. Having some knowledge of persons, organizations, places, and events, he should first consult the printed "finding aids," as the archivists call them, that will tell him the location of various groups or collections. Nearly all repositories are growing, and there are always some sources not yet listed in finding aids. But knowing the kinds of materials that the various institutions acquire will help the researcher to judge where even newly acquired items might be. Thus, he must know something first about the kinds of repositories he may be visiting, and then about the kinds of finding aids that may be available.

The Repositories and How They Grew

The researcher will find a mélange of repositories holding primary source materials, the more so if his subject is broad and his needs extensive. He can hope to find them in an institution that assembles them intelligently, cares for them zealously, and makes them available for study. He may work in a large, well-financed agency that knows its responsibilities and makes its holdings known, or he may have to work in various smaller places, some without facilities for providing more than storage. Sometimes what he wants to use will be still in the hands of the organizations or the individuals that originally filed it; if so, he may or may not be permitted to use it.

To understand this diversity of repositories, one should know something of how it developed (though this is not the place for a history of archives[6]). In the Western world, modern concepts of governmental responsibility for the preservation of valuable records and for their accessibility to the public dates generally from the French Revolution. Then the people began to demand access to records that had previously been closely guarded by the churches or monarchical governments. Most European governments had developed well-organized archives in the eighteenth and nineteenth centuries, with varying degrees of centralized control over the records of local governments. Records necessary to the conduct of daily life and the protection of rights of the individual were kept with increasing thoroughness, usually at places physically close to their points of origin. They included, for example, birth and marriage records, those of lands and debts, wills, inventories of estates, and court records.

In the United States, vital local records were preserved from colonial times by the governmental units involved; those of some state and federal agencies were well preserved, but others received little care. A movement toward central state and federal archival agencies came only in the twentieth century. Establishment of state archives began in the South, soon after the turn of the century, partly stimulated by concern for the history of the Confederacy. Establishment of a national agency was not achieved until the mid-1930's. It resulted from years of effort by historians who were worried about research materials and by administrators concerned about the mass of government records. The National Archives took over the well-ordered archives of major departments such as those of State and War, and has since assembled the historical records of all other agencies.

6. For summaries of archival history, see s.v. "Archives," by Ernst Posner, *Collier's Encyclopedia,* 1962 ed. (New York: Crowell Collier Publishing Co.), 2: 556–57, and by Lester K. Born in *Encyclopaedia Britannica,* 1958 ed. (Chicago: Encyclopaedia Britannica, Inc.) 2: 288–92; and Ernst Posner, "Some Aspects of Archival Development Since the French Revolution," *American Archivist,* 3 (July 1940): 159–72.

Preservation of records of county and other local governments remains subject to many different patterns. What preservation exists has usually been by operating offices such as those of the county clerks and the courts, chiefly because of legal needs, or by state archival agencies or private historical organizations. An important development affecting local records was the Historical Records Survey conducted by the Works Progress Administration during the Depression. Countless records throughout the country were inventoried at that time, and interest in their care was stimulated.

The care of nongovernmental organization records and private papers of individuals and families began with the first historical societies, privately sponsored, in the late eighteenth century. Some individual historians gathered and preserved important papers, but the more widespread collection of nongovernmental sources came later—in the nineteenth century—with the growth of state-supported historical societies, largely in the West. Around 1876, individuals and institutions began to share the centennial fervor for the history of the nation.

Historical societies, libraries, churches, business firms, and countless other organizations have sought to care for the written historical heritage. The leader in gathering and preserving private papers has been the Library of Congress, beginning in 1897 when it set up a special department which has assembled the papers of many Presidents, cabinet officers, and hundreds of other persons as well as associations and other organizations.

An important fact for the researcher is that few of the repositories are limited to any one kind of material. Some operating organizations such as business firms work primarily to preserve their own records. Nearly all institutions, however, and particularly historical societies, universities, state and federal archives, and research libraries, have broader missions. A state archives, for example, will have not only the official records that are its primary concern, but also the papers of individuals active in the state's history.

The collecting activities of most repositories are not limited, in fact, to the dimensions of their sponsoring authorities. They are rather devoted to broad subject fields such as the history of a locality or a state, or even so broad a subject as the history of the West, or perhaps to the history of a certain industry or a certain period. There is another important and quite different dimension in that many of the repositories gather maps, photographic records, and sound recordings that are interwoven with such things as correspondence, and which may have equal archival character.

In this collecting activity, repositories may overlap. One writer has recently said "the possibility exists that some institutions regard manuscript collecting as a branch of intercollegiate athletics and vigorously strive to beat the competition."[7] Ideally, each repository ought to have an avowed field. A number of institutions do cooperate to avoid duplication of fields where it is feasible, but bodies of archives and private papers, especially the latter, seldom pertain exclusively to one area, period, or subject field. Thus, more than one repository may well have a legitimate interest in any lot. The wish of the donor as to where his papers go is usually the controlling factor. The fact is that all repositories working to preserve our documentary heritage cannot possibly provide safe housing for all the valuable records that exist. It is better to have papers preserved in a repository where one might *not* expect to find them than to have them lost to scholarship—supposing, of course, that the repository will care for them and will make its holdings known and available for research.

Since a researcher is likely to have to travel to several institutions if he is working on a broad subject, it behooves him to know what kinds of repositories do exist, what their major fields are, and thus which would be most profitable for him to explore. It may be helpful to provide here a conspectus of the major categories of institutions. It would be even more helpful

7. Walter Rundell, Jr., "To Serve Scholarship," *American Archivist,* 30 (October, 1967): 549. For an entertaining and informative discussion of acquisition fields, see David C. Mearns, "Historical Manuscripts, Including Personal Papers," *Library Trends,* 8 (January, 1957): 313–21.

if they fell into neatly defined and mutually exclusive classes, but that would be too much to expect.

Kinds of Repositories

The variety is seen in the examples mentioned below. They are cited for convenience in terms of their governing authorities, rather than of the types of their holdings. It should be emphasized that they are only examples, and their inclusion does not indicate any kind of evaluation in relation to those that are not mentioned. Such an account could not possibly be a complete listing even of categories; there are hundreds of repositories in the United States alone.

Many of these, existing first to care for the records of the organizations of which they are a part, are properly called archival agencies in the most strict sense. They must give priority in providing information to the offices that create the records, though their devotion to historical scholarship is great. Others, such as research libraries, may perform an archival function in relation to the organizations whose records they hold, though they exist chiefly to collect primary sources for study.

One major category of repositories is made up of governmental archives. For the federal government, the principal element of the National Archives and Records Service is the National Archives, at Washington. It is chiefly devoted to the permanent records of the headquarters offices at the capital, executive, legislative, and judicial; Federal Records Centers in major cities throughout the country care for federal field records; and the National Personnel Records Center at St. Louis houses all federal civilian and military personnel records. Presidential Libraries in New York, Missouri, Kansas, and Iowa, respectively, are also parts of the National Archives and Records Service and are built around the papers of Presidents Franklin D. Roosevelt, Truman, Eisenhower, and Hoover, and collect papers related to their administrations and careers. The other great repository maintained by the federal government is the Manuscript Division of the Library of Congress, already mentioned.

In most of the states at least some archives are open to scholars.[8] State archives are administered by a variety of agencies: departments or commissions especially devoted to historical and archival functions, as in Alabama, North Carolina, and Pennsylvania; independent departments with government records management functions as well as the archives, as in Colorado, Maryland, and Minnesota; state historical societies, as in Kansas, Ohio, and Wisconsin; the secretary of state, as in Georgia, Illinois, and California; the state libraries, as in Connecticut, Tennessee, and Virginia; and fiscal or general services departments, as in Hawaii, New Hampshire, and Washington. One cannot say that any one type of administration always serves the researcher best.

In regard to local records, there has been little change in the historical development already mentioned. Most local records that survive are kept by such operating offices as county clerks, city tax offices, and court clerks. A few state archival agencies, particularly in North Carolina, Maryland, and Delaware, have taken over local archives, and some have microfilmed them. Some local records, fortunately, have been saved by state and local historical societies or by libraries. Few units of local government have provided archival agencies to care for their records, among the exceptions being the cities of Baltimore, New York, and Philadelphia.

Among nongovernmental organizations, examples of business firms that have archival units, usually with records management responsibilities as well, are the American Telephone and Telegraph Company, the Bank of America, the Ford Motor Company, the Goodyear and Firestone Tire companies, and the Denver and Rio Grande Western Railroad Company. A few universities have established separate archival offices, as has Harvard, though most colleges and universities have

8. A thorough and thoughtful analysis of the situation of state archives is given by Ernst Posner in *American State Archives.*

their archives (as well as private papers related to university history) in more general collections attached to their libraries.

Most large religious bodies have repositories of both their own archives and related private papers, varying in part according to the degree of local autonomy in church government. One writer has said that a picture of the location of church records is "like an elaborate patchwork quilt, but without a systematic design."[9] Thus one can mention the Concordia Historical Institute of the Lutheran Church—Missouri Synod, and the American Jewish Archives without suggesting a general pattern.

Countless other organizations, including learned and professional societies and labor unions, have preserved their own archives, and collect related private papers as well.

For those repositories whose major orientation is toward private papers, the private historical societies have been pioneers. The Massachusetts Historical Society was founded in 1791, more than a hundred years before the Manuscript Division of the Library of Congress, and more than a hundred and forty years before the National Archives. It, and other societies established in the nineteenth century, have preserved vast bodies of papers and served innumerable scholars. Among those carrying on this tradition have been the American Antiquarian Society and the Historical Societies of Connecticut, Maryland, and Pennsylvania. The variety of their holdings is endless. Two examples illustrate how the care of archives and private papers is interwoven. The integrity of the Adams family papers at the Massachusetts Historical Society has been so scrupulously kept that they may be considered as family archives, and the same is true of the Cyrus McCormick family papers (which are closely entwined with the history of the McCormick reaper companies) at the Wisconsin State Historical Society.

The difficulty of classifying repositories by their holdings is illustrated by the state-supported historical societies such as those of Kansas, Missouri, and Wisconsin; these have built up

9. Mabel E. Deutrich, "American Church Archives—an Overview," *American Archivist,* 24 (October, 1961): 387–402.

important collections including private papers and organizational records, some of them housing the state archives as indicated previously. This is also true of the great collections of universities (those of Harvard, Michigan, California, and Yale, to name only a few), many of which include the university archives.

Private research libraries are among the most important institutions requiring the attention of the scholar. Some are highly specialized, like the William L. Clements Library at the University of Michigan, which is devoted primarily to the Revolutionary period; many others are quite broad in their subject fields, as are, for example, the Henry E. Huntington Library and the Newberry Library.

County and other local historical societies throughout the country hold countless collections of valuable papers, along with some local government records. They may, naturally, be especially useful to students of local history and to those who need to find materials for study with as little travel as possible. Their care is more likely to be a labor of love on the part of volunteers than that of the larger organizations, and the world of scholarship is forever indebted to them.

Finding Aids

These examples of the manifold variety of repositories should indicate to the researcher that he must be vigilant if he is not to miss opportunities. He will depend heavily upon "finding aids," usually issued by the repositories themselves. It must be noted that most of them are not titled or arranged by the subjects that the student may have in mind. By the nature of unpublished sources, both their arrangement and their volume usually prevent the archivist from satisfying the researcher who would like a published guide to sources on his special subject. This is particularly true with organized bodies of archives, for the archivist is bound to preserve their arrangement and so to list them. This underlines the importance of advance knowledge on the part of the researcher concerning the pertinent organization.

Finding aids fall into several categories for which terminology is fairly well accepted.[10] Researchers will find it useful to consider them according to the degree of detail into which they go in describing the materials. Occasionally the student will find a general work about sources in a broad field, such as the pioneering Van Tyne and Leland *Guide to the . . . Archives of the United States . . .* , the Bemis-Griffin *Guide to the Diplomatic History of the United States,* or the article by Ray A. Billington listing guides to collections useful in American history.[11]

The more usual finding aids are those prepared by the staffs of the institutions for their own holdings. Of these, the broadest in character is the *guide,* which is a description of the entire holdings of a repository or of a number of groups of papers. Guides are usually made expressly for the researcher and may have other titles, such as a list of groups.[12]

10. A more analytical discussion of finding aids, written for the training of archivists rather than for the researcher, is found in Theodore R. Schellenberg, *Modern Archives: Principles and Techniques* (Chicago: University of Chicago Press, 1956), pp. 194–214.

11. Claude H. Van Tyne and Waldo G. Leland, *Guide to the Archives of the Government of the United States in Washington,* 2d ed. (Washington: Carnegie Institution, 1907); Samuel F. Bemis and Grace G. Griffin, *Guide to the Diplomatic History of the United States, 1775–1921* (Washington: Government Printing Office, 1935); and Ray A. Billington, "Guides to American History Manuscript Collections in the United States," *Mississippi Valley Historical Review,* 38 (December, 1951): 467–96.

12. Representative guides issued by repositories are the *Summary Guide to Record Materials in the North Carolina State Archives. Section A. Records of State Agencies* (Raleigh: North Carolina Department of Archives and History, 1963); George P. Hammond and Dale L. Morgan, eds., *A Guide to the Manuscript Collections of the Bancroft Library,* vol. 1 (Berkeley: University of California Press, 1963); and Alice E. Smith, ed., *Guide to the Manuscripts of the Wisconsin State Historical Society* (Madison: Wisconsin State Historical Society, 1944); and Chester V. Kielman, ed., *The University of Texas Archives: A Guide to the Manuscripts Collections in the University of Texas Library* (Austin: University of Texas Press, 1967). Because of the size

An *inventory* carries properly the connotation of accountability of the archivist. He must enumerate the units, be they boxes, file folders, or in small groups even individual documents, to the satisfaction of the donor or the office that transferred them to his care. A *shelf list* is prepared by the archivist primarily for his own use in keeping track of the materials in his care.[13] It may cover all or part of the holdings of a repository, or a specific group. It is designed to show where the boxes or other containers are located, and may list the units within containers such as file folders. Most often it is only a typed list kept in the repository. If it is available to the researcher, it will give him more specific information than the guide.

Both the inventory and the shelf list must describe all the contents of the repository group, accession, or whatever is covered. Therefore they cannot be selective on the basis of usefulness to a researcher (though some units may be more fully described than others). Furthermore, they are closely tied to the physical arrangement of the materials. They are not arranged to suit the need of a researcher as are subject guides, and will contain more that is not useful to him, but they are essential if he is to exploit fully a given body of sources.

The mass of modern records has made it ever more difficult

---

and complexity of their holdings, a single guide to either the Manuscript Division of the Library of Congress or the National Archives is a vast project. The Library of Congress issued a *Handbook of Manuscripts* in 1918, supplemented by a *List of Manuscript Collections in the Library of Congress to 1931,* and a supplement published in the *Annual Report* of the American Historical Association for 1937. The National Archives issued a *Guide to the Records in the National Archives* in 1948, and another comprehensive guide is in preparation. In the meantime, the National Archives has issued a number of guides to records in subject areas, such as the *Guide to Materials on Latin America in the National Archives,* vol. 1, which appeared in 1961, and the *Federal Records of World War II,* 2 vols., 1950–51.

13. Examples of published inventories are the several hundred *Preliminary Inventories* issued by the National Archives and the *Preliminary Inventories* of the Public Archives of Canada. Both series are numbered by record groups. Shelf lists are used by the Federal Records Centers and the presidential libraries of the National Archives and Records Service, among other places.

for the archivist to prepare more detailed finding aids. Occasionally he can make *special lists* or *reference information circulars* that do describe small portions of his holdings by subject,[14] but even so, the interests of researchers vary so widely that these finding aids cannot directly serve each one of them.

Name or subject *indexes* could be made for a fair share of the holdings of some repositories a few years ago, and even now are found occasionally. (For example, the Manuscript Division of the Library of Congress made card indexes of individual documents as time allowed until recent years; now it is turning to automated techniques that will be discussed in chapter 7.) Index cards for names and important subjects have been made for some especially valuable portions of the holdings of the Franklin D. Roosevelt Library, though coverage of all papers there in this way would be out of the question. Where these indexes are found to meet the inquiry of an individual scholar, they are, naturally, of inestimable value to him.

Another type of finding aid that has become increasingly rare on account of the volume and complexities of modern records is the *calendar*. Archivists have sometimes been able to prepare lists of individual documents, item by item, chronologically arranged, and containing summaries of the contents.[15] This required that the items be filed in such clear-cut fashion that they could be listed chronologically without confusion.

Two other kinds of finding aids are frequently useful to the scholar, tools prepared neither for him nor for the archivist in the first place, but for the working office that creates a file.

14. Finding aids built around subjects vary greatly in their scope, nature, and nomenclature. Examples are: Paul Lewinson, comp., *Guide to Documents in the National Archives for Negro Studies* (Washington: National Archives, 1947), and *A Guide to Manuscripts Relating to the American Indian in the Library of the American Philosophical Society* (Philadelphia: American Philosophical Society, 1966).

15. This type of finding aid is illustrated by the *Calendar of Maryland State Papers,* no. 4, pt. 3, *The Red Books* (Annapolis: Hall of Records Commission, 1955), and Grace L. Nute, ed., *Calendar of the American Fur Company's Papers,* pt. 1, *1831–1840;* pt. 2, *1841–1849,* in *Annual Report of the American Historical Association,* 1944, vols. 2–3 (Washington: Government Printing Office, 1945).

One is the *register,* a listing of documents made to keep track of them in current handling. This developed from the English practice in which the registry office controls incoming and outgoing mail and its routing through various offices of an organization. Its counterpart, in less formal terms, in American offices is the log kept of incoming letters with annotations as to what is done with them and when they are answered. This type of listing can be useful to the scholar in finding documents, in tracing their history, and in determining whether or not he has seen all the pertinent material.

The other type of current control device that the researcher will find useful is the *file scheme.* This is so obvious a device that the scholar may not realize its importance. The effectiveness with which the file scheme brings related papers together is not only a measure of the efficiency of the current office, but is also significant to the researcher at a later time. Some file schemes, such as those of the State, War, and Navy departments and the White House, have through the years become quite elaborate. This in itself is evidence of the growth of an organization. (The value of a file scheme is illustrated in a negative way by my experience of finding in the office of a major cabinet minister of a foreign government a filing cabinet in which folders were vaguely labeled and placed with no semblance of order. His secretary had had no instruction or experience in filing. The consternation of a researcher trying to use such a file can be imagined.)

Recent Comprehensive Finding Aids

Two recent major developments are easing the path of the researcher, and deserve his special attention. One is the publication of two important guides covering as far as possible all repositories throughout the United States. The first of these, *A Guide to Manuscripts and Archives in the United States,* edited by Philip M. Hamer for the National Historical Publications Commission and published in 1961, deals with the holdings of 1,300 repositories.[16] There is an entry for each, and they are arranged by cities and towns within state groupings. The entry gives a brief statement of fields of special interest and then mentions the more interesting groups of papers. These are referred to by the names of the persons or organizations from which the groups of papers are derived, with additional information about important persons with whom correspondence is included. The volume is indexed, so that one may find all the repositories that reported holding papers of one individual or organization.

For many years, however, historians and professional associations had been seeking a continuing vehicle for listing archives and private papers in all repositories for the aid of the scholar, bringing out each individual group of papers as they are acquired. At the time of the publication of the Hamer *Guide* there was already in preparation at the Library of Congress the *National Union Catalog of Manuscript Collections,* an adaptation of that institution's National Union Catalog of books. The first volume of "NUCMC" (pronounced "Nucmuc"), as it is known, appeared in 1962, and by 1966 six volumes had appeared, presenting entries covering more than 18,000 collections submitted by more than 600 repositories, with separate indexes indicating items by names, subjects, and places. The entries are published in the order they are received, with no attempt at geographical or other arrangement. NUCMC does not include archives located where one would expect to find them, such as those of a state government in the state archival agency. For this reason "collection" is an appropriate word, referring to "a large group of papers . . . usually having a common source and formed by or around an individual, a family, or a corporate entity, or devoted to a single theme."[17]

Thus, in the Hamer *Guide* the name of Judge Kimbrough Stone appears among those persons mentioned under the entry for the Western Historical Manuscripts Collection at the Uni-

16. (New Haven: Yale University Press, 1961).
17. Library of Congress, *National Union Catalog of Manuscript Collections,* 1966 (Washington: Library of Congress, 1967), p. xvi.

versity of Missouri, and in NUCMC there is a separate entry for Kimbrough Stone, with data about the location, volume, inclusive dates, general character, and conditions of access to his papers. Both approaches are useful.

The other hopeful major development for the scholar is that of finding aids produced by automation. These techniques are now in a period of experimentation, but there are already some tangible products helpful for the researcher. They are discussed further in chapter 7. Many other repositories are experimenting with different applications of data processing cards, and the scholar may expect rapid developments in this field.

Keeping Up to Date

Holdings of repositories are constantly changing as new material becomes available, old papers are brought forth from family storage places, and staffs arrange and list their assets. Thus scholars should be alert to periodic bibliographies, reports, newsletters, and other issuances that discuss recent accessions. Important additions to holdings are mentioned in the news notes of scholarly journals such as the *Journal of American History,* the *American Archivist,* and in the *Newsletter* of the American Historical Association, and are frequently discussed in *Manuscripts* magazine. The Library of Congress notes recent acquisitions of the Manuscript Division in its weekly *Information Bulletin,* as does the National Archives in its journal, *Prologue,* state archival and historical agencies in their official reports, and historical societies in their quarterly magazines. An invaluable listing of finding aids produced by repositories is included in the annual "Writings on Archives, Current Records, and Historical Manuscripts," published since 1943 in the *American Archivist.*

The use of intelligent imagination to visualize what kinds of sources should exist for one's topic has already been mentioned. It cannot be emphasized too much, however, and may well be reviewed again in the light of the preceding discussion of printed materials, kinds of repositories, and finding aids. Let us consider once more the example of Mr. Ascot's gift to Westernland University for a fellowship fund (see p. 12). It may have had such ramifications that it would merit attention in the history of the university, in the biographies of students who benefited from it, or even in the problem of educational financing.

Sources on the Ascot Gift

A researcher studying Mr. Ascot's philanthropy would naturally go first to the printed reports of Westernland University, to a published history of the school if there is one, and to biographical dictionaries. He might even find a biography of Mr. Ascot. Newspaper articles published at the time should tell of the original gift and subsequent awards made to students. Magazine articles might be found on some phase of the subject. All these would not only be informative in themselves, but might also suggest the existence of unpublished sources.

As to archives and papers, the scholar would naturally consult the university archives, hoping to find correspondence, committee files, and financial records. In them he would seek information on the original offer, the acceptance, any supplements to the gift, the policies involved in awarding fellowships, and the actual awards of fellowships to individual students. Private papers of the donor, the university administrators, the professors, and of students who held the fellowships would be useful. They might be held in the library of Westernland University, in those of universities where some of the students may later have had careers as professors, in historical society collections, or in one of the major research libraries. Assuming that the university had to report the sources of its fellowship funds to a government agency, or sought public funds to supplement the original gift, one might find pertinent records in the files of the state budget office or the state education department, hopefully in the state archives. He might be led to the files of the United States Office of Education in the National Archives. Supposing that the Ascot fellowships were significant as an example of the financing of graduate study, there might be information in the files of the Office of Education or in those of congressional committees (also at the National Archives), or in the records of the private foundations that often study these matters. Since there has been considerable public debate over educational financing in recent years, one might well find information on or evaluation of the Ascot fellowships in the private papers of congressmen or of other public figures. The study of financing might involve the sources of Mr. Ascot's own funds, and the records of his own business activities would be pertinent.

With regard to each of these kinds of materials and to each repository, the most direct leads would be the names of persons, or the names of university offices and government agencies concerned with reports, applications for funds, or with research studies. Subjects such as *fellowships* or *education financing* would be useful in referring to file schemes, subject guides, or indexes.

These suggestions are cited simply to show that Mr. Ascot's gift, at first glance a simple matter involving a letter from him to the president of the university and an acceptance, may require ingenuity on the part of the researcher who intends to study it thoroughly.

3

The Researcher and the Archivist

Success in consulting primary sources depends upon the co-operation of the researcher and the archivist. The better the prospective user can explain his needs, and the more clearly he understands the responsibilities of care for the materials, the better the result. The more effectively the archivist carries out his task in terms of the researcher's needs, the more effective the collaboration. A competent archivist is to be looked upon as a scholarly colleague of the researcher, far more than solely a preserver and a caretaker. His knowledge of the sources can contribute materially to the user's evaluation and understanding of them. We may hope that historians will expect more of archivists than one researcher who sent a letter of thanks to this writer (though he meant to be friendly and appreciative) in which, after naming three staff members of the repository, he remarked that "they were more than archivists or librarians—they were genuinely helpful."

In a repository of archives or private papers, the user is bound to be more dependent on the archivist than he is upon the librarian in a library of printed books. The very complexities of the arrangement of loose papers means that finding aids cannot be as explicit or definite as book catalog cards. The uniqueness of primary sources means that they must be handled more cautiously than a book of which other copies can be had if it is lost. Even an experienced researcher cannot expect to "browse" on open shelves of archives or private papers —he would be lost in the maze, and he would be interfering with the archivist's responsibility for protection of his holdings.

What Should Be Expected of the User?

Successful cooperation depends upon an understanding of the basic responsibilities of the archivist for the protection and the integrity of his holdings, duties that sometimes may seem to conflict with his responsibility to aid researchers. Protection implies the assurance that the papers will be kept free from deterioration, careless handling, theft, or physical hazard— particularly fire. Integrity refers to the organic unity of the group, maintained by the archivist as it was created, insofar as possible unaltered, its correlation with other groups indicated, and thus its value as historical evidence preserved. The relationship of one document to others often carries great meaning. Thus in discussing the obligations of the users, there will be stress on maintaining the arrangements of papers.

It is vital that the researcher or inquirer coming to the repository explain his purpose, his qualifications, and what he wants to see. This is true no matter whether he be looking for one fact for a family history, for personal information for legal use such as proof of birth or a social security claim, or for the elements of a major research project. He must understand that the archivist has a responsibility to the government, historical society, or other organization that employs him, and a duty to his profession. Each user is only one of many, and regulations are designed to protect the completeness of the sources and the conditions of study for all.

The user can usually assist both the archivist and himself by writing to a repository in advance, especially if he needs more than quick, one-time service. The advantages of doing so are to give his identification and, more important, to allow the archivist to investigate his holdings to see what he has that might be useful. This survey may spare the researcher a futile trip. (Most repositories require, in addition, letters of introduction from the principal advisers of undergraduate students.)

The statement of needs should be as explicit as possible and in terms that will be helpful to the archivist in consulting file schemes, inventories, and other detailed finding aids. For example, names of persons, dates, names of units of government, accurate titles of organizations or associations, are essential kinds of data. Large topics—for example, housing, civil rights, relations between the United States and another country, waterway control—should be given reasonable bounds such as time periods, names of persons involved, or geographical areas.[1]

The clear phrasing of an inquiry is not difficult for a researcher who has a definite need. In the hypothetical papers of Mr. Ascot at Westernland University (see p. 12) the researcher should easily be able to state which documents he wants to see, and in what files they may be found. (Persons whom archivists do not welcome are those without a clearly defined purpose—for example, the lady who recently called me long distance at the Harry S. Truman Library to say that she was writing a graduate dissertation on the President and to ask, "What can you tell me about him?")

Of course, a student may well visit a repository in the course of his preliminary investigation to find out what topics within a broad field might successfully be studied in terms of available materials. The archivist should be glad to advise him on the basis of knowledge both of existing research and of his holdings; then the student should be prepared to resume his background reading before actually using primary sources.

In most repositories the user will have to apply for a permit or card entitling him to see the materials. In doing this he will normally be asked to provide the following information, either in an application form or an interview:

Address (both home and local)
Institutional affiliation (for a graduate student or faculty member, the university where he is based; for a staff

1. Professor Philip D. Jordan makes a good case for "fishing" by the experienced researcher without being required to state his intent precisely, and also laments "picayunish, police-type" regulations, in his delightful article, "The Scholar and the Archivist—a Partnership," *American Archivist,* 31 (1968): 57–65. He recognizes the need for the elements of cooperation stated in this manual, with a human touch.

researcher from a nonacademic entity, the firm or
agency represented)

Position (for a graduate student, whether M.A. or Ph.D.
candidate; for a staff researcher or faculty member, his
title or rank)

Previous research experience or publication

Topic of study and kinds of materials needed

Expected length of study at repository

Publication plans

These data will enable the archivist to issue the accrediting
permit. They will also guide him as to the kind and amount
of assistance that the researcher may need, and the actual materials that should be produced. Those in charge of collections
often develop a keen interest in the productive work of their
clients, but in these identifying questions they are not just ex-
ercising curiosity. They are carrying out definite responsibilities. The archivist can reasonably expect the researcher to understand those responsibilities, and to comply with rules based
upon them.

In order to become an accredited researcher, the scholar
will probably be asked to sign a statement that he will observe the research room rules. These rules are designed both
to protect the integrity of the documents and to assure good
working conditions for all users. They normally include the
following:

1. The user is to sign for the items that are entrusted to
   him—(usually by folder titles, boxes, or other unit rather
   than by individual items).
2. The user must share the responsibility of keeping the
   papers intact and in good order.
3. Negatively, the user must observe the following:
   a) He may not smoke. (This is primarily to protect the
       papers from fire, but is also to make the room more
       comfortable for other researchers.)
   b) He may not use ink, though ballpoint pens are gen-
       erally permitted. (The hazard to the papers from

possible spilling or smearing of ink must be avoided.)

c) He must not damage the papers by writing on them, leaning, or tracing over them; by folding them other than the way they were found; by placing paper clips or rubber bands on them; or otherwise. He must take special care of fragile papers.

d) He must not destroy the arrangement of the papers, neither individually nor by folders, as he finds it. If he rearranges them for his own purposes, he will be destroying the evidential value of their original arrangement for other users. If they become disarranged, he must allow the archivist to restore their order rather than attempting to do it himself.

4. He should promote good working conditions for all by observing rules as to quietness, and he should not take up the time of the other users or of the archivist by conversations in the research room except for necessary consultation about the papers or their contents. Even though the conversation may be legitimate scholarly debate, rather than about the latest baseball game, it may disturb others who wish to concentrate upon their work. The use of typewriters or dictating machines is determined by local "ground rules," depending upon the amount of disturbance they may cause.

5. He must not remove papers from the research room. Because papers have been stolen from repositories, it is only fair that they be used in the presence of a member of the staff at all times, not in a private study or other place. Archivists are not happy to impose this condition on mature users, but they cannot otherwise assure the integrity of their holdings (and a user who seems quite mature could be the most mature thief). For the same reason, the researcher will in many repositories be asked to submit his brief case or other packages for inspection.

6. He should always inform himself as to his responsibilities regarding permission to quote or publish the contents of documents. The responsibility is almost always his rather than the archivist's (see chap. 4).

The archivist has many kinds of clients and many kinds of problems. Not only does he have the obligation of his employment to serve graduate students and post-graduate scholars, but he is equally bound to assist professional and amateur non-academic writers, genealogists, lawyers, private citizens with claims against a government, and many other users. In a government archives, reference service for official business has to come first. The fact that his recent, voluminous collections are largely unbound accentuates the difficulty of keeping track of individual papers. And in an institution of any size he is likely to have administrative duties as well as those of service to researchers.

Among the administrative worries of the staff of an institution, one of the most immediate involves the hours of work. Most researchers understand that very few institutions can provide adequate service and protection of their holdings in more than normal office hours. This is admittedly a problem for traveling researchers having limited time in one place; regrettably, they will be fortunate if they find repositories that can afford to pay staff members to provide reference service on weekends, and they will rarely find one that can enable them to work in evenings.

What Should Be Expected of the Archivist?

There are obligations that the archivist can reasonably be expected to fulfill, just as the user should follow the rules given above.[2] The accredited researcher can expect the archivist to take his project seriously and to devote earnest effort to producing materials that will be useful. It is the duty of the archivist to bring the pertinent papers to the researcher's attention and to provide such information about them as cannot be found elsewhere. The user may expect this explanation to include basic data on the file scheme or arrangement of the papers,

2. The basic principles are set forth in "The Archivist's Code" [prepared by Wayne C. Grover and members of the staff of the National Archives and Records Service], *American Archivist,* 18 (1955): 307–8.

their relation to the body from which they came, and some background about persons, offices, and the like insofar as it cannot be had in available reference books. The archivist may well explain the meaning of file symbols, the position of an official of a government in relation to his superior, the source of a body of papers if it is not apparent, or why the position of a certain company officer would make him an especially good witness to some event. But the user ought to find for himself the history of a government agency, the major biographical details concerning an individual, the organizational structure of a company, and the general nature of an event or transaction when that information appears in published reference books or is apparent in the content of the papers themselves. This all pertains to a question sometimes asked, "Who does the work?" The user cannot expect the archivist to do his research for him, but he can expect reasonable and competent assistance.

The archivist's explanation of the primary sources is important for more than just easing the researcher's path. The essence of the archivist's care for the integrity of his holdings, in fact, is to provide the user sufficient data as to the source and identification of a document, and sufficient assurance that it has not been tampered with, so that it may be accepted as valid evidence.

Much has been written about the historian's criticism of his evidence. Both the archivist's careful work and his knowledge of the sources are vital to the scholar in this respect—in fact, the scholar is wholly dependent upon the archivist not only for the preservation, the condition, and the order of the documents, but also for their identification. And the more thoroughly the archivist has studied his holdings, especially for description and publication, the more help he can be to the user.

The archivist should be expected to suggest to the user other sources than those about which he originally asked. It often happens that the person in charge of a collection knows of items that bear on a user's topic. In fact, a competent archivist should, and generally does, know his collection well enough to provide invaluable leads of this kind.

At the same time, one who uses papers in a repository should be given access to some kind of finding aids so that he can judge for himself what groups or series might be useful to him. While the nature of guides, inventories, shelf lists, and other descriptive items varies widely, some basic listing of the collections should be at hand. (I have a painful memory of working for weeks in a major foreign archives where no inventories were made available to the researchers, only to have the archivist in charge call my attention just a few days before the end of my stay to a bundle of papers that formed the core of my whole study.)

Adequate facilities may be expected, but the extent to which they are comfortable will vary with the circumstances and the resources of the repository. Professors of European or American diplomatic history have long enjoyed regaling their students with tales of the rigors of work, for example, in some of the more remote Spanish archives. Conditions in some records storage places in Washington sixty years ago, or even less, appear to have been worse. These form a contrast to the present concept of what a repository ought to provide in the way of well-arranged and -lighted research rooms, staffed by competent archivists, with the useful complements of good reference-book collections, microfilm readers, and reproduction facilities nearby. But the extent to which a user will find typewriters available to obviate carrying his own, coffee shops at hand, and smoking rooms nearby depends on the degree of his good fortune.

"Processing" operations, which include initial examination, whatever arrangement is necessary, review to determine the application of donor agreements or other possible limitations on access, boxing, shelving, labeling, and listing in finding aids are necessary and take considerable time. While the researcher should recognize these necessities, he can expect the archivist to schedule them so as to aid users as quickly as possible. There have been many examples of papers that are inaccessible simply because this internal work has not been done. The competent archivist avoids such situations.

Helpful suggestions are often made to researchers by archivists about primary sources in other repositories or in private hands. Many repositories keep files of such information as part of their specialized knowledge relating to their main fields of research. The researcher may well expect such assistance, especially in a repository with highly concentrated holdings in a certain time period or geographical area. While repositories sometimes compete for acquisitions of bodies of papers, they seldom impede a researcher's work by failing to tell him of papers that have been deposited elsewhere.

Cautions

Patience is a requisite for successful research, and its need is certainly illustrated in the use of primary sources. For example, one may feel frustrated by finding only parts of the information he seeks in one body of papers of one repository. This is especially true in studying recent decades, but even for earlier times, the problem exists. One studying the life of a Forty-niner in California might have to search in various parts of the East for letters that he wrote to members of his family describing his experiences, and for records of his West Coast activities in repositories there. While for a period so long past the repository staff may have had an opportunity to make name indexes more completely than for recent times, there are likely to be papers pertaining to our early-day miner in several groups within one institution—even parts of correspondence with one other person may have become separated, despite the wishes of the archivist to have related papers together.

For recent periods, this problem looms even larger. Complexities of organizations, greater mobility of people, and the intricacies of file schemes often result in the papers relating to one activity being found in several different groups within a repository, or in several different locations. A researcher studying a problem of modern Indian affairs, for example, might find material in the records of the Office of Indian Affairs in the National Archives, in the private papers of a former Commissioner in the Library of Congress, in a report made to the president in a presidential library, in local government records of the area concerned, or in private family correspondence in a historical society, and perhaps in other places which would be identified only by painstaking search. There are practically no topics of major research (that is, say, of the scope of a doctoral dissertation) that can be studied adequately in one repository of papers.

Not only should the scholar be willing to search for and use all the pertinent materials, but he should also be imaginative as to information that might appear in sources for which no leads might appear. The study of a battle, for example, may depend upon the weather conditions prevailing at the time. Accounts by participants in letters or diaries may vary, but scholars have found the official records of the Weather Bureau surprisingly informative about specific days and localities in years past.

Some users expect to see, and to need, only outstanding single documents, such as the letters between two famous statesmen, the original drafts of a speech, or the final plans for the reconstruction of a church. They are likely to be disappointed either because the key documents are not available for some reason, or because those few items do not contain the explanations, the "whys" that the student should really be looking for. Thus these users tend to scorn the mass of documentation as meaningless and useless. They illustrate the kind of researcher who does not appreciate the manifold problems of access to papers (especially recent ones), or simply does not want to take the trouble to work out the full account of a development from the numerous records that contain parts of the evidence.

Another temptation of the student is to be so carried away by one document or one account of an event that he does not steel himself to look further. The fact that one correspondent, or one diarist, seems to have a particularly vivid or full narration of events, or that he was the highest level official involved, does not necessarily mean that the scholar can rest there. Often there are other papers relating to the same subject, perhaps by a lesser official, one at the "working level," that may provide balance or be even more informative. Thus the exploitation of the primary sources is not complete when one has found an unusually satisfying bit of evidence—or one that agrees with his own hypothesis.

Nor can one feel that his search at a given time is definitive. All things must end, and this is especially true of the doctoral dissertation. But until the deadline arrives, the scholar must be prepared for the occasional discovery of new materials and changes in the holdings of repositories. A really live institution, with the realization that its worth in the future will be judged by the quality of its holdings, is always on the alert to build up its collections. The circumstances that determine at what time a given collection of private papers is given to a repository, for example, are widely varied and follow no schedule. The holdings of active repositories are constantly changing. This is recognized by both archivists and users as a problem for which there is no ideal answer.

It is impossible for the institution to inform all users of every bit of evidence it acquires currently on every subject. The archivist has an obligation to inform the scholarly world generally of its acquisitions, and to keep its finding aids as up to date as possible. But the researcher can never be wholly certain that a repository will not acquire vital papers on his particular topic just after he has finished his research there. The only solutions to this dilemma are for the student to keep himself informed on announcements of acquisitions by repositories, and for the archivists to issue even quite general and brief announcements of acquisitions at the earliest opportunity.

Special caution must be stated regarding use of archival repositories by mail. The general rule is that the repository will give information about its holdings by mail, will answer specific questions as to whether or not it has material on a given subject, and will provide information on specific inquiries that is readily available from its holdings without extensive study. But this brings us back to the question, Who does the work? The archivist may have to do somewhat more for an inquirer by mail than for the researcher who comes in person, but he should not be expected to do extensive work, or make any interpretation for him. Most institutions will provide the names of professional researchers who will do work for persons at a distance, and some limit the amount that the archivist will do by setting a specific time limit on the search he will perform.

But there are other difficulties that make it unfeasible for a researcher to expect by mail more than information about sources or answers to specific questions. By mail, repository officials cannot as easily learn the qualifications and purposes of the researcher as if he were present in person, and thus they may justifiably be more reluctant to make information available if there are problems involved. The inquirer surely cannot explain his needs as fully by mail as he can in person. He cannot explore marginal possibilities as readily, and he cannot judge the usefulness of material without seeing it. Thus any substantial study demands a visit to the repository in person.

Propriety Regarding Other Users

Propriety guides the relationship of the researcher and the archivist to other users. The practice of withholding material that a particular scholar is using is now outmoded. Many historians in the past have had their priority in the use of certain papers protected by the archivist, who would not show them to anyone else. Some university archivists, particularly, still occasionally withhold from general use materials that certain faculty members are using. This practice probably derives from the days when the historian collected materials himself and hoarded them for his own use—many priceless collections have been preserved for posterity only through the zeal of such scholars. But today, most of the preservation of sources is done by the various kinds of repositories discussed in chapter 2, rather than by individuals, and such repositories must represent the interests of all potential users. The current policy of most archival institutions is that a scholar may expect privacy as to the details of his own work, but not exclusive access to sources. Thus, most archivists feel that what is open to one user should be open to all (those institutions with a public responsibility, such as government archives, *must* follow this policy), and materials withheld should be only those upon which certain restrictions apply (as will be discussed in the next chapter).

The archivist should protect the researcher's work to the extent that he does not tell others in detail what documents the researcher is using or the way in which he is developing his theme. The researcher has reason to assume that as a matter of propriety the staffs of repositories will avoid disclosures, in idle conversation or otherwise, that would give away the product of thought and time that the researcher has invested in his own work.

Avoidance of work duplication by mentioning the topics of other scholar's work, however, is normal procedure. Several publications serve this end (for example, the American Historical Association's triennial *List of Doctoral Dissertations in History in Progress*), but a broad subject can often be worked over productively by two or more researchers, often emphasizing different sources to bring out their conclusions. This is increasingly true as the plethora of unpublished sources increases. Professors usually guide their graduate students, however, in selecting dissertation topics so that their findings will be unique. I, for example, had the experience of learning after the completion of my basic research in several foreign and American repositories that another student, from another university, had much the same project underway, using many of the same materials. No archivist, American or foreign, had mentioned the duplication. Fortunately by a gentleman's agreement the other student changed his topic slightly and used the same research for a highly commended book. But such an incident could seriously upset a student's program, and this kind of dilemma can better be resolved before it arises than after.

4

Limitations on Access and Use

It might well be that three scholars would seek to use correspondence of three American Army generals, one of the Revolution, one of World War I, and one of the Korean War, and that archivists would have the unpleasant duty of declining all three requests. Papers of the Revolutionary War hero might be withheld from use because of their fragile condition; those of the World War I figure because his family had placed restrictions on them when they were given to an archives; and those of the Korean War leader because they were security classified. This hypothetical but easily possible situation illustrates some of the complex reasons why researchers occasionally cannot see the sources they would like to use.

The archivist realizes that in order to preserve the sources and to live up to his duty to the authorities from which he got them he may occasionally either prevent or delay legitimate research. Thus he regards control of access as one of his most serious responsibilities. He seldom has complete freedom of choice in his decisions. The user need not expect to put up with the rare stubbornness of a custodian who withholds documents on account of some whim, but he will sometimes have to accept restrictions on use, and he should be told the reasons for them.

Physical Protection of the Documents

Limitations that the researcher will meet are of two general kinds, those imposed because of physical hazard to the documents, and those that pertain to their content. In the first class we naturally think of rare old papers, such as letters of the Revolutionary War period, usually in one of the great private treasure houses like the Huntington Library or the William L. Clements Library.[1] One can easily study the content of most of these documents by using facsimile copies or published versions. The rare scholar who needs to analyze the actual paper or some other physical features of the document itself must be highly qualified and must exercise extreme care. Only a scientist or archivist concerned with the physical condition of the original of the Declaration of Independence would ever expect to see it outside of its helium-filled glass "sandwich" in the National Archives exhibition hall, but its contents have been read by countless students from facsimiles, published versions, or just poor copies. Of course many fragile documents have not been reproduced or published, and the archivist responsible for their care naturally has to consider the hazards of use.

A more modern corollary of this problem arises not because of the value of the documents, but because the physical medium is poor. For example, at the Franklin D. Roosevelt Library, some papers of the 1930's have become fragile through use and are being replaced by facsimiles for current study. At the Dwight D. Eisenhower Library, facsimiles made by certain processes and found among the files are having to be replaced because they are susceptible to fading or smudging. These problems are common to many repositories, and nothing is more flimsy than the tissue copy of an outgoing letter.

Limitations on Content

The second broad category of limitations applies to the information contained in an item, rather than to its physical state. We are speaking here of sources containing information which could be used against some valid public or private interest. In

1. Jean Preston, "Problems in the Use of Manuscripts," *American Archivist*, 28 (1965): 367–79.

order to understand the bars to access to such items we must ask whether the reasons for creation of the documents entail any obligations to open them to researchers, the extent to which they are available if still held by the organization or person that created or filed them, and why they are sometimes not available in archival repositories. Later in this chapter we shall discuss the limitations that one may encounter in citing, copying, or quoting from the sources.

Why Are Documents Created?

Most people write letters, memorandums, or other kinds of documents for current purposes, and do not consciously create historical sources. Only a small portion of those accumulated really have lasting informational value. And only if there is a public interest involved is there any real obligation ever to make them available to scholars. Nearly every human organization has its scribe, however, who sets down the record for future use. It may be presumed that what he writes is intended to be consulted by someone at a later time.

The obligation to let researchers see the documents (aside from needs of disclosure for certain legal purposes) varies from those few governmental organizations that have specific requirements to that effect, to private persons who have no obligation to let anyone see their correspondence unless they wish to do so. Thus a researcher is more likely to see the records of a government in a public archival repository than he is to see private papers still in the hands of a family; and there are many degrees between these two extremes.

United States Government Records

Probably no organization in this country has done more to make its records available than the United States government; probably none is more maligned by scholars for the limitations that do exist. The principle that a government should keep records developed naturally as an administrative necessity. In this country, the responsibility to keep records was inherited from colonial and European practice. As the government grew, its agencies kept records, often by administrative direction. But there was no general requirement that they do so until the Federal Records Act of 1950.[2]

The concept of availability of records to the public was put forth by the Puritans, and was recognized in Europe at the time of the French Revolution.[3] As to allowing scholars to study the records, there was the example of the French Revolutionary laws, and the somewhat ambiguous concept of the "public records," applying largely to legal and fiscal purposes.[4] But such precedents as there were did not assure access to the working files, correspondence, memorandums, and countless other items that often tell researchers the "whys" they seek about governmental decisions and actions. The State and War departments and a few other agencies had their own archives providing reference service to scholars, and the National Archives was established in 1934 to serve that purpose for the federal government in general. An extensive reference service was developed then, but there was no general requirement that federal records be made available, to scholars as well as others, until the Freedom of Information Act of 1966.[5]

Much of the basis for use of government records lies in the principle of the people's right to know, which most people think of as applying primarily to the release of information in the press. In signing the Freedom of Information Act, President Lyndon B. Johnson said:

> This legislation springs from one of our most essential principles: a democracy works best when the people have

2. Federal Records Act of 1950, Sec. 506, 64 Stat. 586.

3. Ernst Posner, "Some Aspects of Archival Development since the French Revolution," *American Archivist,* 3 (1940): 159–72.

4. Oliver W. Holmes, " 'Public Records'—Who Knows What They Are?" *American Archivist,* 23 (1960): 3–26.

5. Freedom of Information Act, 1966, 80 Stat. 250.

all the information that the security of the Nation permits. No one should be able to pull curtains of secrecy around decisions which can be revealed without injury to the public interest.[6]

The citizen rightly expects his government to provide information that he needs for his personal rights, such as data on his social security account, his veteran's benefits, and the like. But as a "stockholder" in his government, he also has a right to know why and how it has acted in certain ways. This is the concept of accountability to the governed that must guide all democratic governments.

The Freedom of Information Act puts the emphasis in legislation upon the availability of federal records, unless specific conditions of restraint exist, rather than upon the disclosure of information only to persons directly concerned with the subject of inquiry. It stipulates that government agencies should make available certain classes of opinions and orders; more important for the researcher, it stipulates that they should open all other records upon reasonable description by the applicant of the records he wishes to see, subject to certain exemptions.

President Johnson, continuing his statement at the signing of the bill, explained:

> At the same time, the welfare of the Nation or the rights of individuals may require that some documents not be made available. As long as threats to peace exist, for example, there must be military secrets. A citizen must be able in confidence to complain to his Government and to provide information . . . without fear of reprisal or of being required to reveal or discuss his sources. Fairness to individuals also requires that information accumulated in personnel files be protected from disclosure. Offi-

6. Lyndon B. Johnson, "Statement of the President upon Signing Bill Revising Public Information Provisions of the Administrative Procedure Act, July 4, 1966," *Public Papers of the Presidents of the United States, Lyndon B. Johnson, 1966* (Washington: Government Printing Office, 1967), p. 699.

cials within the Government must be able to communicate with one another fully and frankly without publicity.[7]

The exemptions were definitely stated in the Act as

applicable to matters that are (1) specifically required by Executive order to be kept secret in the interest of national defense or foreign policy; (2) related solely to the internal personnel rules and practices of any agency; (3) specifically exempted from disclosure by statute; (4) trade secrets and commercial or financial information obtained from any person and privileged or confidential; (5) inter-agency or intra-agency memorandums or letters which would not be available by law to a private party in litigation with the agency; (6) personnel and medical files and similar files the disclosure of which would constitute a clearly unwarranted invasion of personal privacy; (7) investigatory files compiled for law enforcement purposes except to the extent available by law to a private party; (8) contained in or related to the examination, operating, or condition reports prepared by, on behalf of, or for the use of any agency responsible for the regulation or supervision of financial institutions; and (9) geological and geophysical information and data (including maps) concerning wells.[8]

Security Classified Records

By far most of the records that scholars might wish in vain to see relate to national defense or foreign policy. Caution in these fields is by no means new. Military and diplomatic activities by nature have always had to be conducted in some secrecy.

Throughout history military and diplomatic officials have marked documents as "confidential," "secret," or some other

7. *Ibid.*
8. Freedom of Information Act, 1966, 80 Stat. 250.

such designation. The first statutory basis for the security classification of records in the United States came in the Espionage Act of 1917, which provided penalties for improper handling of government records.[9] This was strengthened in 1938 by legislation to prohibit the making of a photograph, map, or sketch of any vital military or naval installations or equipment; a Presidential proclamation of 1940 defined that phrase to include many kinds of records.

These provisions applied only to the military, but during World War II many other government agencies became involved in the war effort. By a succession of presidential orders they obtained the authority to mark documents as "security classified." Agencies that would normally be concerned with strictly civilian duties were involved in research, information, finance, supply, and countless other government operations that were part of the conduct of the war.

Rules for identifying the categories of security classified documents ("restricted, confidential, secret, and top secret") and their handling proliferated. Presidential orders and agency directives emphasized the need to avoid overclassification. These cautions were difficult to define or enforce, however, and it was inevitable that some things were classified for reasons other than security. Many were legitimately security-classified but for considerations that were only temporary, such as press releases before their issue, budget-planning documents, and itineraries of high officials. Security regulations included provisions for downgrading and declassification, but until after the Korean War emphasis was put upon security rather than upon access to records.

The kaleidoscope of security regulations was clarified in Executive Order 10290 of September 24, 1951. In issuing it, President Truman said that "the American people have a fundamental right to information about their government." He cautioned against classification for other than grounds of national defense, and the order urged downgrading when possible. Executive Order 10501, of President Eisenhower, Novem-

9. Espionage Act of 1917, 40 Stat. 217–31, as amended.

ber 5, 1953, limited the authority to classify documents to agencies having direct responsibility for the national defense.[10]

Removal of Security Classifications

Most security regulations state that only the officials who initially classified documents or their successors may change security classifications. This often makes changes difficult to secure, especially when time brings changes in personnel and organizations. Some relief was provided by Executive Order 10964, of President Kennedy, September 20, 1961, which included a schedule for automatic downgrading; by rulings of the Attorney General; and by the efforts of agency and archival officials.[11] In particular, the Department of Defense has designated officials to work on this problem. That department's Directive 5200.9, for example, on September 27, 1958, declassified the great bulk of its records dated before 1946. Later the department initiated a plan of automatic one-step downgrading ("top secret" to "secret," "secret" to "confidential," for example) every three years. The directive could not, however, guarantee that the holders of copies of the documents would change the security markings accordingly. The National Archives at the same time, either by applying such blanket authorizations to portions of its holdings or by the much more time-consuming process of consulting agencies regarding specific documents, has worked to lift barriers to research as rapidly as possible.

Another avenue of access lies in the granting of clearances to individual scholars to use items that are still classified. The General Services Administration has set up a procedure in which the National Archives will handle applications of scholars for clearances, though in many cases applications for access must be made to the agencies as well. A researcher who has reason to think that information he needs exists in records

10. Executive Orders No. 10290 and No. 10501, 3 CFR 1949–1953 comp.

11. Executive Order No. 10964, 3 CFR 1959–1963.

that are still classified should consult the National Archives regarding possible clearances.

Orders issued by the Department of the Army cover documents which the originating offices believe should be safeguarded even though they do not contain defense information. They are stamped "For official use only," and if a date of termination is not included with the stamp, that limitation expires in three years.[12]

Records of Foreign Affairs

Like military records, those of foreign relations have been generally exempt from the general trend toward public access that has grown since the French Revolution. At the same time, governments have bolstered their positions at home and abroad by publishing selected portions of their diplomatic correspondence. Thus many countries have through the years issued series analogous to the Department of State's *Foreign Relations* and its various predecessor series.

The scholar may expect a cautious policy in the opening of the mass of records not published in *Foreign Relations* to researchers from outside the government. In the United States, diplomatic records are opened earlier than in most foreign countries. This writer had the experience before World War II of seeking access to records in a European country covering relations with the United States more than a century before. The files of the foreign office, which had been transferred to the national archives, were open but those of the legation in Washington, kept in the foreign office archives, were still closed. While practices of various governments vary widely, it is common to close records for fifty years or more. A committee of the International Council on Archives is working for the reduction of these periods of time.

The Department of State has three periods applying to access by nonofficial researchers. Records more than thirty years old are open, and are in the National Archives. There is a

12. Army Regulation No. 345–15, June 30, 1967.

"restricted" period, from thirty years up to the publication of the latest volumes of *Foreign Relations*; this has usually been something over twenty years. Files dated since that publication are closed. The department has a procedure, through its Historical Office, for the handling of applications for access to records in the restricted period. Access for research, according to the statement of the Historical Office, is granted "as liberally as possible, consistent with the national interest, the maintenance of friendly relations with other nations, the efficient operation of the Department and the Foreign Service, and the administrative feasibility of servicing requests."[13] Of course, the department has records that are security-classified in the strict sense, as well as those that have been labeled as confidential on a less formal basis according to practice of many decades standing. The regulations cited above cover all types of materials.

The Departments of State and Defense have primary responsibility for records in the first category of those exempted from the terms of the Freedom of Information Act of 1966. Many other agencies have security-classified records, however, and their problems and practices are similar to those of the Department of Defense in lesser degree. Limitations on access are exercised in most agencies by designated officers to whom the scholar should make application to see files still in agency custody. He can learn who they are by consulting the National Archives. The researcher may expect that time and the conscious efforts of many officials in charge of records will minimize the bars that confront him, and that records of lasting value will probably be transferred to an element of the National Archives and Records Service before he wishes to use them.

Records in Federal Archival Custody

The Federal Records Act of 1950 provides that the Administrator of General Services (who has delegated the authority to

13. "Availability of Records of the Department of State," June 28, 1967, 22 CFR § 6.9.

the Archivist of the United States) shall administer any statutory restrictions on the use of records transferred to the National Archives, as well as restrictions stated in writing by the head of the agency transferring the records.[14] This provision applies also to records of research value in the Federal Records Centers. The act says, however, that all restrictions on records more than fifty years old will be automatically removed unless the Administrator for some special reason orders that they should remain in force longer.

A series of restrictions sheets (the "pink sheets") are available stating what limitations apply to the various groups of records and by what authority they have been imposed. Most record groups carry no restrictions at all. "General" restrictions apply to a few categories, such as immigration and naturalization records of individuals (a statutory restriction), medical records less than seventy-five years old pertaining to individuals, and records less than seventy-five years old pertaining to investigations of individuals by various authorities. Restrictions applying to specific record groups include, for example, those of closed sessions of Senate committees; Treasury Department records pertaining to relief to banks through the Reconstruction Finance Corporation; all records of the Department of Justice less than twenty-five years old, with certain exceptions; military personnel records; and others.

Personal Papers in Federal Custody—Presidential Libraries

Papers in the presidential libraries of the National Archives and Records Service are for the most part personal, in the legal sense that while they may be the archives of individuals or offices they are not official records of the government. Thus they are handled in accordance chiefly with limitations on access stated by the donors in instruments of gift rather than by the rules governing federal records. The libraries are authorized to accept "the papers and other historical materials of any President or former President of the United States, or of any other official or former official of the government, and any other pa-

14. Federal Records Act of 1950, Sec. 507, 64 Stat. 587.

pers relating to and contemporary with any President or former President . . . subject to restrictions agreeable to the Administrator as to their use."[15] The act further states that these papers and other historical materials shall be held subject to such restrictions ". . . as may be stated in writing by the donors or depositors."

All the presidents, from George Washington on, have regarded their papers as personal. No feasible way has been found to segregate what might in a stricter sense be called official, political, and personal as they accumulate. Furthermore, no president is likely to agree to immediate use of his papers. "Every now and then," W. Kaye Lamb, Dominion Archivist of Canada, has said,

> someone proposes that it should be made compulsory for cabinet ministers and the like to hand over their papers to the Public Archives, and to do this promptly on retiring from office. To my mind this policy is quite impracticable and, if put into force, would fail to produce the desired result. Unless they were assured of some measure of protection, most of the people concerned would simply destroy their papers, and no one could stop them from doing so. In addition, I think the policy might well prevent much interesting material from coming into existence, for the tendency would be to put as little as possible on paper.[16]

These remarks apply with even more force to the papers of the presidents of the United States.

The bodies of presidential papers in the presidential libraries are analogous in kind to those of many earlier presidents held by the Library of Congress. The papers of Presidents Roosevelt, Truman, Eisenhower, and Hoover in their respective libraries are covered by instruments of gift that vary in wording but in general provide for the closing of broad categories of

15. Presidential Libraries Act, 1955, 69 Stat. 695–97.

16. W. Kaye Lamb, "The Archivist and the Historian," *American Historical Review,* 68 (1963): 387–88.

papers, rather than individual documents, and other donors have followed suit.[17] These categories include items which might be used to embarrass, harass, or damage any living individual or that might jeopardize the conduct of current foreign relations; those that relate to family business or personal affairs; and of course those that are security-classified. In applying these stipulations, the library officials must have all the papers reviewed, and must bear in mind general principles of privacy and propriety. The Archivist of the United States has the authority to lift restrictions on specific documents or series when the reason for closing them has passed. Thus there is the dual responsibility of observing legal obligations to the persons from whom the papers came, and of making as much as possible available for research. Some donors other than the presidents have stipulated that their papers may be used only with their permission, but they are in the minority. Unlike most repositories holding personal papers, the presidential libraries do not "screen" applicants for research, although they are authorized to turn away applicants who do not have a serious purpose. The general policy is that papers open to one are open to all, and the great majority of papers in the libraries are open.

The Library of Congress

Papers in the Library of Congress are also for the most part personal rather than official records, and some are subject to donor restrictions and considerations of national security. In fact the practices of the Library of Congress are more similar to those of most nongovernmental repositories than are those of the presidential libraries.

The reasons for restrictions by donors naturally vary with

17. This statement does not apply to the Rutherford B. Hayes Library, at Fremont, Ohio. Since it is not a federal government agency, it is not subject to the discussion of restrictions immediately following. The Hayes presidential papers are subject only to "library restrictions," like those of many other repositories, requiring that users be qualified researchers. The age of the papers makes restrictions unnecessary.

individuals, but generally involve matters of personal caution or privacy, and the feeling that correspondence involving other persons should be respected. The limitations are usually stated, however, in terms of permission to use a whole collection, and require a request to the donor. Thus there is an opportunity to consider the purposes and the character of the applicant for access.

All the papers of the presidents of the United States in the Library of Congress are free of limitations on access. The majority of other groups of papers in that depository bear no restrictions; they exist only on some quite recent materials. Researchers wishing to use papers in the Manuscript Division will find some information about limitations in the *National Union Catalog of Manuscripts,* but should inquire of the Chief of the Manuscript Division as to their specific needs.

Unauthorized Use of Closed Documents

One aspect of the circumstances applying to closed documents, especially of the federal government, amounts to the taking of an unfair advantage by some authors (at the same time it works to make available information that would otherwise remain restricted). That is the occasional practice of government officials of taking copies of closed documents with them, among their personal papers, when they leave office. There is nothing to prevent their taking their own copies of government records, but the taking of copies of security-classified documents is a breach of regulations. Many eminent persons have written memoirs based in part upon such documents, creating an anomaly for the archivist, who has been carefully guarding copies of the same documents subject to the control of the creating agency.

State and Local Records

Limitations on the use of records of state and local governments constitute no such problems as those in the federal government, largely for the reason that there are no matters of foreign relations or national security to consider. The states follow no uniform pattern in legislation governing the use of records, though most of them require that certain materials pertaining to public expenditures and other specified matters be considered "public records" in the sense of being available for inspection by the citizens. Laws governing particular operations of state agencies sometimes require that related records be confidential, but such rulings are more often made by administrative orders of state officials.

Most state archives laws do not authorize agencies to stipulate restrictions upon records that they deposit in the archives. On the contrary, agencies are likely to hold records that they believe should not be opened until the reasons for confidentiality have passed. The supposition that records in the state archives are there to be consulted by scholars is evident in the conclusion reached by Dr. Posner after making his pioneering survey of state archives, that general legislation includes among the archivist's duties in handling the records "to grant reasonable access to them to scholars, students, and other qualified persons."[18]

Archivists in charge of historical records of state governments, whether they be in official archives or in quasi-official units such as historical societies, are nearly all responsible for keeping also the archives of private organizations and the papers of individuals. In that capacity they operate on donor restrictions, if any, much like those at the Library of Congress.

The circumstances as to freedom of access for the scholar to records of local governments defy any orderly description. Few local governments have official archives, and it is a question how many fully support the people's right to know. This democratic principle is expressed in many county and city charters, and the fact that local governments are responsible for taxation, utilities, education, and other matters affecting the daily lives of the citizens makes for the observance of the legal concept of "public records": taxpayers want to know how their

18. Ernst Posner, *American State Archives,* p. 311.

money is spent. But how far this goes toward helping the scholar who wishes to learn the "why" in correspondence, memorandums, and other "working files" is problematical.

Organizational Records

Universities, churches, business firms, professional associations, labor unions, and the many other kinds of organizations like those mentioned in chapter 2 follow no uniform rules and are generally not bound by laws either in the keeping of records or in making them available to the public. They accumulate files largely for the conduct of their current business, and it is among the management responsibilities of their executives to determine how those records are handled. How conscious such executives are of that responsibility varies with organizations and with individual officials. Increasingly, business firms, universities, and research organizations are involved in government contracts, the terms of which stipulate certain recordkeeping practices. In some cases these will involve security classification just as with agencies of the government itself.

Researchers are likely to find records most accessible in those organizations that have established their own archives and employed competent persons to operate them. Here the concept of an archives as preserving records for a purpose other than that of their immediate creation helps the scholar. Possibly the strongest factor in causing organizations to allow access to their records is that of public relations. This is especially true of business firms.[19] Officials of firms and institutions often feel, and usually rightly so, that their "image" is improved if their story is told. The researcher who is writing the history of an organization for or in association with it may expect broad access to its records (though he may not get it; even universities have been known to "sit on" certain files).

For the scholar seeking information for other kinds of stud-

19. Gerald T. White, "The Business Historian and His Sources," *American Archivist,* 30 (1967): 19–31.

ies than company histories, however, such as biographical or regional research, the story may be different. It may be supposed that a quasi-public type of organization such as a university will be more liberal than a private business, and that older records will be more accessible than recent ones. But there is no general pattern. The researcher can only hope that the organization has set up an effective archives, or has transferred its records to an archival repository outside its own organization.

Papers of Individuals

A large category of sources has not been treated in this discussion of sources in the custody of the federal government, records of state and local governments, and those of private organizations. The correspondence and other papers of individuals, whether they be former public officials or not, make up the bulk of the holdings of the hundreds of repositories referred to in chapter 2, and these have not been dealt with in our treatment of limitations.

The individual citizen is even more free of obligation to keep papers and to make them available to others than are nonofficial organizations. To be sure, the individual must keep financial records that support his income tax returns, and there are other legal requirements, but they are almost all within the realm of personal business records. No one is required to keep a diary, or to retain the letters he receives. If he does, he is under no obligation to show them to anyone (except to the courts in case of certain kinds of legal actions, which affect a minute portion of all personal papers). If an individual or his family, realizing that his career or his writings may be of lasting interest, chooses to preserve his papers and to give them to an archival agency, the donors have the right to protect their own legitimate privacy by stipulating the conditions under which the papers may be used.

Scholars may sometimes use personal papers while they are

still in the possession of the families or individuals concerned. If so, they are naturally subject only to the conditions laid down by the owners—which may entail an understanding that only a favorable treatment of the subject is intended.

For the most part, however, the owners of historically interesting papers will give the responsibility of providing reference service on them to an archival institution of some kind. Considering the manifold types of repositories referred to in chapter 2, the prospective user should expect a wide variety of policies.

Limitations on use are most often exercised in two ways already alluded to: the "screening" of research applicants, or screening of the papers, as is done in the presidential libraries. The American Historical Association's Ad Hoc Committee on Manuscripts in 1950 preferred the screening of applicants, and discouraged donor restrictions. It found a wide divergence of practice in response to a questionnaire it used, and concluded:

> Some sort of screening of applicants for permission to consult recent papers is felt by this committee to be desirable. Part of a sentence or a paragraph from a confidential letter written, perhaps, by someone still very much alive, if lifted out of context, spread on the front page of a yellow journal or quoted in false context at one or more of our more lurid public hearings, not only causes sober scholars to shudder, but may also, understandably, cause prospective donors of valuable papers to decline to become actual donors. And scholarship will thereafter suffer.[20]

The screening recommended by the committee involved the use of questions such as those set forth in chapter 3 regarding the approach of the researcher to the archives. The more conservative the archivist, the more will he be restrictive in his judgment of the applicant's qualifications and the validity of

20. Report of the Ad Hoc Committee on Manuscripts, *Proceedings of the American Historical Association, 1950* (Washington: Government Printing Office, 1951), pp. 68–69.

his project.[21] Archivists are concerned about the preparation of the applicant in having read the printed material on their subjects first, and may hope that they do not have to spend too much time showing the student how to use unpublished sources.

Most repositories do accept papers with donor restrictions, and feel it essential that they do so.[22] This is often a requirement in their negotiation with a prospective donor, and donors must be assured that the stipulations will be strictly observed. Else, as implied in the Ad Hoc Committee report quoted above, there may be fewer papers coming to the repository. Restrictions may be stated as requirements that the donor's permission be obtained for use; that users meet certain qualifications; in terms of a period of years for which the papers will be closed; or by citation of a contingency that must pass before they are opened, such as the completion of a biographical project. Some archival institutions withhold general access until a particular scholar has completed his project; a few university archivists, for example, will give exclusive access to certain papers to a faculty member. Fortunately, this practice is becoming less common than it was formerly.

In Favor of the User

This discussion of limitations on access may cause the researcher to ask, "What, then, is on the side of the user?" There is a great deal on his side. Most important is the fact that the majority of sources in archival repositories are available for use despite these problems. Another recourse lies in

21. Useful discussions of this kind of "screening" appear in Jean Preston, "Problems in the Use of Manuscripts," and Howard H. Peckham, "Policies Regarding the Use of Manuscripts," *Library Trends,* 5 (1957): 361–68.

22. For further discussions of donor restrictions see W. Kaye Lamb, "The Archivist and the Historian," Jean Preston, "Problems in the Use of Manuscripts," and Ruth B. Bordin and Robert M. Warner, *The Modern Manuscript Library* (New York: Scarecrow Press, 1966), pp. 74–78.

finding the information sought elsewhere than in the place one encountered bars to access. Considering the plethora of copies that are often made of documents, some may be found in closed groups of papers and some in completely open groups —this has happened more than once within a single repository. The same thing sometimes happens among files of an agency that have not yet been transferred to an archives. What is required is ingenuity and persistence on the part of the user.

Most archivists are idealists concerning their obligation to serve research and will make papers available if it can be done. Most government archivists are conscious of the principles evoked in the Freedom of Information Act of 1966, even though they may not know of that act or it may not apply directly to them.

People and organizations generally have some sense of history, and want to preserve information for posterity (despite the often-quoted question, "What has posterity done for me?"). This desire applies with special strength when posterity is viewed as the future generations of a family, or those who will carry on a business firm. Many persons realize that the sources should not only be preserved, but should be made available to those who will understand and explain the travails and the accomplishments of the present generation. The element of vanity is a strong motive. Individuals often want those who come after them to be aware of their merits, and to appreciate the problems they have met. For similar reasons, their descendants, wanting their family stories told but not knowing how to go about it, may give access to papers to experienced researchers. This motive counters the natural reluctance many have to let strangers "poke around" in their personal affairs.

This writer has had enough experience on the user's side to understand the frustrations that limitations on access can cause. Not only was he unable to see in a foreign country certain records more than a century old, but he had to submit for review at the Department of State the notes he took on files of a negotiation that took place over 110 years before. He is at some loss to see how the review of notes can control what a scholar writes, and fortunately such stipulations are less common today than in years past. Until recently this writer could not see certain files of his father because the House of Representatives closes its records for fifty years. Other papers of his father are in a repository where they may not be used without permission of the donor. And certain of his own files in the records of an emergency agency of government are still security-classified, though twenty years old. Memory suggests that little if anything in them can still be really "sensitive." The comment comes to mind of a government military historian, fully entitled to handle highly classified documents, who said somewhat wistfully, "I wish I *did* know a military secret."

Yet experience as an archivist, responsible at various times for sources limited for all the grounds described, shows that there are truly serious reasons why cautions must be observed. We may hope that researchers understand that fact even if they do not have to be burdened by the sometimes complex reasons involved; and we also hope that archivists will be broad-minded, realizing that it is basic to the scholar's task to see every bit of evidence that he can.

May I Quote or Copy?

Obtaining permission to see or to read an item may not mean that the user's problems are entirely solved. He will often want to cite or to quote a document, or to reproduce it entirely. He should be informed of the general practices in this regard: the accepted policy of repositories is "let the user beware." With some care, however, the scholar will meet little real difficulty.

The researcher may assume that if he can see a document he is free to cite it—else it would not be open to him. Only very rarely will he be told that he can look at something but will not be permitted to say he has done so. As to quotations, most of them will be short enough to be covered by the rather ambiguous concept of "fair use" (discussed below). One of the few bars the user is really likely to encounter is in the reproduction of a text in which someone has a monetary interest (the necessary permission for short quotations can usually be obtained). The other restraint that may confront the researcher is in the use of a quotation that would justifiably offend or injure someone, and that can usually be avoided by the application of good judgment.

The first time a researcher is likely to encounter these problems is when he asks for copies from an archival repository. He will probably receive notice that it is up to him to obtain the permissions that may be necessary for the use of his copies in anything he writes and publishes. This is true of papers, and especially of photographs. The archivist can in most cases tell him if permission is necessary and from whom it is to be obtained. No government agency is allowed to copy a security-classified document, even though a scholar may have obtained clearance to see it. A few donors of personal papers stipulate in their instruments of gift that their permission is necessary for the copying of their papers. Some repositories, including the Library of Congress, will not without the donor's permission make copies of documents upon which the donor has retained literary property rights.

The law of literary property is involved in definition and in its interpretations down the years to the extent that only a bold layman would attempt to define the principle. In general it protects the author of a writing, not the physical document but his creation in the composition, from unauthorized publication by someone else.[23] It is rarely actually invoked in law, and then it is applied usually only to compositions of such literary content that they may have a monetary value in publication and sale. It is not generally pertinent in business correspondence, in forms that are filled out, or in official documents. One who writes a memorandum or letter on official business of the United States government, or a letter to a government agency on the business of that agency, has no literary property rights in the writing.

23. Philip Wittenberg, *The Law of Literary Property* (Cleveland: World Publishing Co., 1957), pp. 59–76.

Most correspondence and memoranda, in fact, do not have
the kind of quality that involves literary rights. But public
figures, professional men and women, travelers, journalists,
and other writers often produce interesting letters, essays,
speeches, and other manuscripts that could profitably be published, and they can claim the exclusive right to do so. They
do not have to take any definite action (such as the registration of a copyright to a published work) to secure this right.

The right to exclusive control and publication may be inherited, assigned, or otherwise legally transferred. In fact, one
of the strongest factors protecting the research user is the frequent practice of archival agencies to persuade the donors to
transfer their rights to the repository or to the public. This
is done in the Library of Congress by having the donor, if he
is willing, assign his rights to the public; in the presidential
libraries, by having the rights transferred to the government;
in other repositories, by having them transferred to the historical
society or other authority to which the repository belongs. But
the donor is always entitled to yield the physical possession of
the papers and the control of their use for research, and still
to retain the literary rights—just as a person can sell land but
retain the mineral rights in its future exploration. Even so, any
collection of personal papers is likely to contain letters written
by persons other than the donor. These persons, and their heirs,
own the literary property rights in their writings.

Copyright established by statute may be thought of as applying to published materials, whereas literary rights are a matter
of common law applying to unpublished writings. But the two
items are closely related, and legislation that has been pending
in Congress for some years would bring them even closer.

Fair Use

Countering the researcher's concern over literary property
rights is the protection of the doctrine of "fair use," a generally
understood but never clearly defined rule of thumb. The courts

have recognized that it is fair to quote a reasonable portion
of even a copyrighted work for use in research, criticism, review,
or summary. This means that by such use a person does not
infringe upon the owner's rights enough to impair the value
of the work as a salable property. Those responsible for the care
of unpublished materials generally recognize the same principle
with regard to archives and private papers. They will advise
a researcher that he must get permission to use in print more
than fifty words, or three lines, or one of various other suggested limits. But it is still the responsibility of the user to
decide what he will use and to obtain any permission that is
felt necessary.

A Case in Point

We should not leave the student of Mr. Ascot's fellowship gift
to Westernland University too long without attention. His success in getting at materials will surely vary with the length
of time that has passed since the period that he is studying.
By the time the fellowships have been established long enough
to merit research, most of the pertinent papers should be open.
The personal correspondence of Mr. Ascot and of the professors who held Ascot fellowships when they were graduate
students may have been placed in university archival collections
or other repositories. Whether or not they carry donor restrictions depends largely on their personalities and that of their
families. The business records of Mr. Ascot's company (the
company through which he made the money that he gave to
the university) are likely to be closed because they represent
commercial interests in competitive industry; but we may hope
that they would be opened in twenty-five years or so. Committee and business records of the university should be in
its archives, and open to researchers. The files of lawyers
involved in the donation may be the hardest to reach, as they
represent the confidential relationship of an individual or firm
to its counsel. Reports of income furnished to government
agencies by the university should be open, as it may be assumed

that the institution has a tax-exempt status for donations. The income tax returns of students who received fellowships, if their incomes were large enough to be taxable, would probably have been disposed of by the government agency concerned. Records of state or federal agencies, such as offices of education, should be accessible in the appropriate archives. Those of private foundations that conducted studies of educational financing might be closed for some years because they contain information furnished in confidence. Accessibility of legislative records would depend upon the practices of the state legislatures or the federal House and Senate; the accessibility of the papers of individual legislators would depend on the idiosyncrasies of the members themselves.

5

Notes and Copies

We have said that the user must carry knowledge to the archives, and we know that with care and effort he can carry knowledge away with him. But for practical purposes he must take away something more tangible in the form of notes or copies. The transition from his reading of the sources in the repository to his use of what he has found after he has gone home involves some problems more complex than he faces in using other types of materials. Decisions as to what notes to take, how much to copy in full, and the methods of this work will affect the value of his study, the amount of time he spends, and the accuracy of his references and quotations.

Notetaking

There is a happy medium in notetaking. The researcher must, of course, have enough information in writing so that he does not depend on memory for factual items or quotations. But he should not measure the success of his research by the quantity of his notes. One professor whom this writer knew felt sure that he was making progress because he had accumulated ten thousand cards full of notes. He was an exaggerated example of the researcher who becomes enamored of details of unknown value, and loses sight of his broad objective. The minimum must be enough notes and of sufficient quality to make his citations and quotations accurate, to guide other scholars who wish to use the same sources, and to enable the archivist to find the same items in case the scholar needs to consult them again. There are many ways of taking notes, and several textbooks on historical method that present suggestions.[1]

Whatever the method of note-taking, the researcher using unpublished primary sources should indicate the repository where he has found his material; the group or body of archives or private papers concerned; the series within the group, if any; the exact identity of the item used; and the substance of interest to him. The user's notes will usually follow the reverse order of an eventual footnote citation. For example, a letter relating to Mr. Ascot's fellowship gift would be noted first by the repository, say the Westernland University Archives; then the group, probably the papers of Samuel F. Ascot; the series, outgoing letters; and last the item identified by kind, persons involved, and date. This last might be "letter, Ascot to Pres. Addison Lamb, Jan. 14, 1926." After that, an abstract or summary of the content, or the quotation, that made the letter worth citing: "Initial offer of gift for fellowship. SFA specified conditions of use of funds. . . ." Thus, with the broader headings first, several specific notes on series or items can be entered under one general entry for the repository. While abbreviations will naturally be used freely, it is essential that the first note for each repository, group, and series give the precise title in full, just as it is used by the repository.

A user is likely to visit an archival repository only occasionally, and its holdings are by definition unique. He cannot easily go back to certain items at will, as he could go back to a book of which copies appear in many libraries. Therefore it is important that he record just what groups he looked at, how thoroughly he examined them, what further materials he would have studied if he had had more time, and other facts for

1. For example, Homer C. Hockett, *The Critical Method in Historical Research and Writing* (New York: Macmillan Co., 1960), pp. 134–42; Louis Gottschalk, *Understanding History: A Primer of Historical Method* (New York: Alfred A. Knopf, 1966), pp. 73–85; Wood Gray et al., *Historian's Handbook,* 2d ed. (Boston: Houghton Mifflin Co., 1956), pp. 54–56.

his own future reference. The chronological scope and the arrangement of the materials should be noted, and the researcher should indicate whether he checked all of a group or only part of it. Items which one expects to use will naturally be noted fully, but often some general indication of those series which proved irrelevant or useless is helpful. The scholar should not have to depend on his memory as to whether he has seen them or not.

It is useful to note the name of the archivist with whom one has dealt in a repository. That person will take an interest in the researcher, will develop an understanding of his project, and will probably bear it in mind in case other materials appear. Even though the personnel of an archival institution changes from time to time, references to individuals dealt with are often helpful.

One should err on the side of inclusion in taking notes, for much greater time would be required to return to a repository at some distance to obtain information that one had failed to record than would be needed to put down a few additional notes while there. For example, in the sequence of correspondence between Mr. Ascot and President Lamb, a letter that did not appear at first to bear on the fellowship gift might later prove to be important. Or, after writing about that particular donation the scholar might choose to treat a closely related problem, and notes taken generously could be useful. Many an article of importance has been written by a scholar who kept alert for interesting ancillary information and noted it while he was in the repository and had the opportunity. In the long run, only the researcher himself can make the judgment of how much to record in his notes.

One of the worst errors a scholar can make is to approach an archival institution with a preconceived notion about his subject so firm that he takes notes only on those bits of evidence that support it. Prejudices are likely to be rigid; hypotheses need to be tested, and the scholar might easily change his views in such a way that what he first thought useless would become significant. Or he might be charged by others with not having seen certain materials, and should be able to defend himself. Thus the apparently mechanical matter of notetaking involves broader concepts of the objectivity and the thoroughness of research.

Footnotes

Although an essayist once decried footnotes as irritants "that run along the bottom of each page, like little dogs barking at the text,"[2] they are the means by which an author shows the authority for his statements or quotations. Archives and private papers are more complex in their identification than printed books, and therefore the accuracy of footnotes to them in publication is even more critical. The order of footnotes is normally the reverse of that in the notes that a user takes for his own study. The first reference in a footnote is to the individual item, and the series, group, and repository follow. The example cited above, for instance, would probably be written as "Samuel F. Ascot to Pres. Addison Lamb, Jan. 14, 1926, Ascot Papers, Outgoing letters, Westernland University Archives."

Rules of style, punctuation, and other details of footnotes will be specified by publishers. Archival institutions, however, frequently issue instructions to ensure the best manner of referring to their holdings. Advice given to researchers by the Harry S. Truman Library, for instance, suggests that:

> A citation should identify the particular item used, the group in which it is filed, and this Library. The item should be identified as to type, name, file location if necessary, and date. While other helpful information should be given, in general, citations should be simple.[3]

2. Rev. Samuel Crothers, quoted in Charles Warren to Felix Frankfurter, Nov. 19, 1941, Charles Warren Papers, Manuscript Division, Library of Congress.
3. Harry S. Truman Library, Instruction leaflet, "Citations to Research Materials in the Harry S. Truman Library" (Independence, Mo.: 1966).

Ten sample citations are then given, representing various kinds of series and items. Among them are:

> Charles S. Murphy to Samuel J. Smith, Dec. 16, 1950. Civil Rights folder, Murphy Files, Truman Library.

> Report, Civil Rights Committee, Sept. 14, 1947. Records of Civil Rights Committee, Truman Library.

> Speech, Harry S. Truman, Des Moines, Iowa, Sept. 14, 1948, PPF4, Truman Papers, Truman Library.

> Draft, Speech for American Legion Convention, Sept. 14, 1948, Murphy Files, Truman Library.

> Telegram, National Wildlife Association to Oscar L. Chapman, Sept. 29, 1951, Conservation folder, Chapman Papers, Truman Library.

The actual content of footnotes varies, of course, according to the circumstances. Examples representing quite different kinds of materials from those referred to above, but still following the sequence from the item to the repository, are given in the *Style Sheet* of the Institute of Early American History and Culture. "Consistency," says this issuance, "may be the hobgoblin of little minds, but not in matters of style." Among the examples it gives are the following:

> Thomas Jones to Richard Lee, London, July 5, 1755, Richard Lee Papers, XXI, 29, Old Colony Historical Society, Taunton, Mass.

> William Blathwayt to Treasurer Godolphin, Feb. 17, 1707, Treasury Group, Class 64, Piece 89, 393. Public Record Office.

> Timothy Pickering to John Marshall, Sept. 20, 1798, Domestic Correspondence, XI, 98, Record Group 59, National Archives.

In these examples, the class or group numbers are usually those assigned by the archival agency. "R.G.59" at the National Archives, for example, refers to Record Group 59, comprising the records of the Department of State.[4]

Copying

Often a user needs to refer to or quote so much of a document, or will need to study it so thoroughly, that he is warranted in having the whole item copied. He should realize that while methods of copying have improved immeasurably and the cost has been greatly reduced in recent decades, copying involves care, time, and expense to him and can be a burden to the archivist. Thus again there is a happy medium to be sought. The scholar can spend a disproportionate amount of his time, his funds, and even his filing space in proliferating copies, while at the same time he can enhance the ease and the accuracy of his future use by having exact copies of the necessary items.

Many of today's older scholars have laboriously copied documents by longhand or by typewriter in their own research, or employed other persons to do it for them, with a considerable attendant possibility of error. Photographic reproduction has changed all that within a generation. Most repositories provide copying facilities or have them accessible, and a few scholars carry their own reproducing machines with them. These means have eased the process and increased the quantity one can afford to have copied, as well as reducing the likelihood of error.

In fact this improvement in itself provides a temptation for the researcher. There can be a great difference in the quantities if he copies only those documents he is likely to cite or quote, if he obtains a larger volume to peruse at leisure in his home or study, or if he is collecting everything he can get on a subject. We are talking here about the scholar who is copying

4. Institute of Early American History and Culture, *Style Sheet for Authors* (Williamsburg, Va.: Institute of Early American History and Culture, 1968), pp. 1, 12, 13.

for his own use. Items so chosen are not apt to be valuable for deposit in another institution, such as his own university, because they are incomplete and cannot well serve researchers on other topics.

Another choice is necessary, that of the method of copying. Most repositories now provide facilities for producing both microfilm and full-sized facsimiles. Microfilm is generally best for a large number of documents in sequence. Technical developments in this field are rapid and the machines used vary widely; this is not the place for an analysis of them. Microfilm is far less expensive per item than facsimiles, and it has the advantage of small compass and ease of carrying or shipping. But microfilm requires the use of reading machines. Occasionally people find it difficult or tiring to use microfilm readers, but they have been developed to a point where one should be able to use film freely. Microfilm reproductions are usually on a roll film and cannot be sorted, rearranged, or annotated as can facsimile pages. Microcopies of single images on film or paper stock have been developed, but up to now are used far less than roll film.

Machines for making facsimiles, meaning full-size paper copies, are usually best for the copying of selected items not in sequence, and are also changing rapidly. The quality of copies, ease of use, permanence, and cost vary widely. The researcher should avoid the use of "quick-copy" devices that do not produce permanent images. They are satisfactory for current use in offices, but since the copies fade, they will not serve the researcher's long-time need. Facsimile copies do have the great advantages that they can be filed with other papers, marked up, arranged in various ways, and if they are of good quality can be read as easily as typed pages for many years.

These are technical problems of which the user should be aware, particularly the choice between microfilm and facsimiles, so that he will know he is getting copies adequate for his needs. He can depend on the staffs of larger archival agencies to advise him on these matters. An archival institution is not likely to have more than one kind of equipment of each type, however, so the user may not have a choice.

Costs of copying services vary from one institution to another and from time to time. The general range is from five cents up for each image or "frame" of microfilm, and from ten to fifty cents each for facsimiles, sometimes differing with the quantity ordered. The researcher should be informed of the prices before he orders, since the probable costs may seriously affect the kind and amount of his order.

Copying makes problems for the archivist, in addition to those of literary property rights discussed in the previous chapter. His basic responsibility for preservation of the sources makes him cautious about exposing his holdings to the handling and light—which might damage the documents—necessary for copying. The copying is normally done by a technician in a laboratory apart from the research room, and the documents must therefore be withdrawn from use by other scholars while the work is being done. In a large repository, and when a user orders a large quantity of copies, this can be a real problem. The procedure necessary for the identification, protection, and actual copying of the materials can be a substantial workload for the archivist. This is particularly true in fields such as genealogical study, where one user may make frequent orders of large quantities. Some archival institutions have had to set limits to the number of items they will copy for a single user in a stated period of time.

Indicating the items to be copied is a procedural step on which the repositories necessarily have precise rules. This must be done in such a way as not to damage the documents (as paper clips would), and to preserve their order. Their identity must be clear at all times, both so that the technician can properly label them (usually by photographing an identification slip with the document) as to their group and series, and so that they can be returned to their places accurately and quickly.

Other technical problems will arise from time to time. Oversize documents usually cannot be handled on rapid-copy machines. Maps and charts must also be separately handled, probably by regular photography. Photographic prints or pictures in newspaper clippings will not reproduce well on the copying devices. Researchers who wish to use their own copying machines must assure the archivist that they will not damage or disarrange the documents, will not expose them to light that might fade them, will not use liquid developers in the repository, and will not interfere with the work of other researchers.

Special problems are met when copies are ordered by mail, especially if the requester has not visited the repository. For instance, identification of items is more difficult than if done in person, even though the scholar may give good general descriptions of what he wants. The archivist dreads a request like one received at a repository from a graduate student who named a rather broad topic and said: "Please send me twenty dollars worth of material on this subject." The copies were not, of course, provided without a more specific order.

A "blanket" order for all the items in a repository on a subject or person for the use of an individual scholar, as for example one might order all the letters of Mr. Ascot in the Westernland University Archives, is likely to put an unfair burden on the archivist, who must save part of his time for other users. Furthermore, Dr. Howard Peckham of the William L. Clements Library has written: "Such requests are generally regarded as stretching library and archival courtesy . . . the feeling prevails that such scholars are leaning too heavily on another person's judgment. . . . They are missing the thrill of discovery. And they are failing to perceive the tangential relations that are often illuminated by a chance remark buried in an inconsequential paper. It may be argued that such scholars are pursuing research without catching up to it."[5]

5. Howard H. Peckham, "Policies Regarding the Use of Manuscripts," *Library Trends,* 5 (January, 1957): 364.

6

Criticism of Modern Unpublished Sources

"Get your facts first," Mark Twain once advised Rudyard Kipling, "and then you can distort 'em as much as you please."[1] This admonition suggests the relationship of the archivist to the researcher, though it would not meet with the approval of professors of historical method. For in getting the facts from documents, the scholar must first identify the documents, and in that task he can expect aid from the archivist. What the researcher does with the facts, in evaluation or interpretation, is his own responsibility.

External Criticism

The scholar's first step in the use of a document is to ascertain by whom it was written, where, and when, and under what circumstances. Then he can proceed to study its content. The concept of historical criticism in these two phases, referred to by somewhat varying definitions as external and internal criticism, respectively, was developed largely by the late nineteenth-century German historians, who also stressed the growing emphasis upon the use of archives in research.[2] One

1. Rudyard Kipling, *From Sea to Sea: Letters of Travel* (New York: Charles Scribner's Sons, 1909), 2: 282.
2. Ernst Bernheim, *Lehrbuch der historischen Methode und der Geschichtsphilosophie,* 3d ed. (Leipzig: Verlag von Duncher und Humblot, 1903), pp. 300–503; Charles V. Langlois and Charles Seignobos, *Introduction to the Study of History* (New York: Henry Holt & Co., 1898), pp. 71–140; Allen Johnson, *The Historian and Historical Evidence* (New York: Charles Scribner's Sons, 1926), pp. 50–100.

American author defined external criticism as dealing with the document, whereas internal criticism has to do with the statement.[3] Our emphasis here will be on the first of the two, as it is the more pertinent to problems in the use of archives. The cooperation of the archivist and the user in this respect is one of the best illustrations of the role of the archivist as a scholarly colleague of the researcher.

When a user has papers set before him by an archivist, he can expect them to be identified as to the person or office with which they originated, as to type, name of series, and date span. The labeling of a box of papers as the outgoing correspondence of Mr. Ascot for the year 1926 provides a large part of the identification that is needed. Furthermore, the person in charge of materials has an obligation to assure the user that they are exactly as he received them, complete, in the same order, and as nearly as possible in the same condition. This duty naturally varies in degree from, say, the amateur archivist of a local historical society who has simply inherited the papers from predecessors of many decades and cares for them as a labor of love, to the professional archivist within a government organization who is responsible for the whole "life history" of the records of that unit. From the latter, the user can reasonably expect much more assistance than from the former.

Authorship

Determination of origin is vital to the historian in understanding the authority, special interests, and other characteristics that a document represents, as well as the steps in procedure through which it has gone. This may depend upon several factors other than the obvious one of the author's signature. An unsigned paper may often be identified by the handwriting. The researcher who is doing an extensive study of one of

3. Homer C. Hockett, *The Critical Method in Historical Research and Writing* (New York: Macmillan Co., 1960), pp. 13–82. Both Hockett and Louis Gottschalk, *Understanding History: A Primer of Historical Method* (New York: Alfred A. Knopf, 1950), pp. 118–71, discuss problems of criticism and cite many examples.

several principal figures should learn his handwriting. This is the kind of problem on which an experienced archivist, with his thorough knowledge of the documents, can be helpful. The researcher may regret the apparent decline in the teaching of penmanship, as well as the role of the professional longhand copyist, yet the reduced use of longhand makes him less liable to have to identify and decipher the handwriting of certain notable figures such as, for example, Horace Greeley—whose penmanship was wretched.

Memorandums of government and business in recent decades have often been identified only by initials, or—far worse for the historian—by the symbols of organizational units. Only a thorough knowledge of the administrative history of the organization one is studying will make it possible to identify either the authors or the recipients of these papers. Once the individual who wrote a document has been identified, the researcher will want to learn his place in an organization, his function, and his immediate activity at the time the paper in question was created. This kind of information may be at hand from the preliminary study of printed sources urged in chapter 2 of this manual, and the more that is true, the more quickly and easily can the user profit by study of the sources. But new names and organizational units are constantly turning up. Archivists frequently preserve organization charts and directories that are invaluable in this connection.

The "organization man" of the twentieth century works largely in offices, committees, teams, and "task forces," whether he be in a private institution, a business firm, or in any unit of government. Some critics of large organizations complain that this tendency makes it difficult to assign responsibility for decisions (though they suggest no feasible alternatives). Certainly it increases the difficulty for the historian in determining the origin of documents, and—even more important—the origin of the ideas that they represent. The scholar studying recent periods must simply accept this as a way of life, and be prepared to deal with it. High officials are likely to have assistants who draft documents, "ghostwrite" them, or revise them. Sometimes those persons identify themselves (either to share the responsibility or to claim credit), but frequently they exercise a "passion for anonymity." These circumstances call upon the skill of the researcher to apply his critical faculties, his knowledge of the organization, his study of the style of writing and trains of thought of principal persons, and other clues to tell him how and from whom statements have developed. He can look, for example, for successive drafts and for marginal notes on them.

Perhaps the most exciting examples of these problems involve the public statements of high government officials. Books have been written largely devoted to the evolution of the "Truman Doctrine" speech of President Harry S. Truman to the Congress on March 12, 1947, regarding aid to Greece and Turkey, and the Harvard Commencement address of Secretary of State George C. Marshall of June 5, 1947, in which he proposed what became known as the Marshall Plan.[4] Memorandums, drafts, and other documents in the Harry S. Truman Library, the Department of State, the George C. Marshall Research Library, and other places bear on these subjects, as do other published works. The truth is probably that no single person wrote all of either speech, and that in each case the man who finally delivered it initially outlined the main elements and was responsible for the final wording. But what ideas and wording came from which participants, and what debates took place over them, will intrigue historians for years to come.

Similar problems on various scales of complexity and significance often face the researcher. Papers of members of staffs of the presidents, of other offices at all levels of government, and of persons in industry and private organizations hold countless memorandums, suggestions, and drafts to provide challenges to scholars. The student of Mr. Ascot's donation to Westernland University would be interested in the policy development involved in the wording of the announcement to students that the fellowships were available. The same is true of the drafting of legislation, of policy statements of all

4. Joseph M. Jones, *The Fifteen Weeks* (New York: Viking Press, 1955); and Ellen Garwood, *Will Clayton: A Short Biography* (Austin: University of Texas Press, 1958).

kinds of boards and committees, and other issuances for the public. In any of these cases the scholar may find unsigned, undated, or unlabeled contributing items.

Dating of Documents

One aspect of external criticism which the historian will encounter and in which continued archival custody is significant is the dating of sources. Well-organized and continuous files, in which time periods are clear, comprise a larger share of the historians' evidence for recent decades than for the nineteenth century and before, though people will probably always be careless about dating letters and memorandums that they write. Students of earlier periods are more likely to encounter private papers of which the provenance is not wholly clear. There are methods of establishing dates, however, some open to the researcher himself and some in which he must consult the technicians. He can tell, for example, if a letter about life in Oklahoma was written before or after 1907 according to whether it speaks of the area as Indian Territory or as a state; often references to well-known events or the style of writing will be informative in this connection. Even the history of the sources themselves, including the fact that certain documents were deposited in an archival institution before or after a certain time may tell something as to when they were created.

Modern scientific techniques make it possible to tell the age of paper quite closely. The kind and condition of ink used in writing or printing can be analyzed with valuable results. These techniques are usually not available to the individual scholar, and not likely to be applied unless the documents and their dates are unusually important and other methods of identification have failed.

Variant Sources

The scholar often finds more than one copy of a document among the sources. Until the development of the most modern electrostatic copying methods, it could be said that no two copies of a paper were exactly alike. Variations in the physical appearance of the paper, errors in copying by hand, and notations put upon different copies of the same document when they went through various stages of procedure or to different recipients all made at least slight differences that could be detected by comparison. It is often the task of the historian to determine which is the "original" or the authentic copy, in the sense of being the first one written or the one agreed to if there were some sort of compact. The same problem sometimes arises as to which draft of a speech was actually presented. Until recent decades, for example, treaties with foreign governments were written out in longhand by professional penmen, at least one copy being made for each country. Especially in the early days of the Republic, duplicate copies were sent to assure that at least one reached its destination. Still other copies were exchanged when the treaties were ratified. The treaty files of the Department of State, for example, contain three signed copies of the Treaty of 1819 with Spain. The same duplication occurred with most diplomatic papers. Almost inevitably there were small differences in the wording as copied. Sometimes these variations have led to diplomatic disputes and more often to the confusion of historians.

To take a more recent situation, by the time of World War II the federal government had grown to the point that several different agencies as well as one or more foreign countries, might be involved in one transaction concerning supplies to be delivered abroad. The writer remembers seeing a procurement form that was made out in thirty-three copies, most of which went to different places, received different entries, and became parts of widely separated files. Were they copies of the same record by the time the process was complete, or originals each in its own way?

Of the innumerable copies of documents made for research purposes, as distinguished from those made for current use in the creating offices, the fact that they were copies could until recently be easily observed. It could be seen they were photographic prints, that the paper differed, or some other difference of appearance was evident. In recent years, however, processes have come into use that make copies on any kind of paper look the same as that of the original. Often the color of the printing in the original and the copy are not easily distinguished, though a typed letter with a signature in ink can be told from the original in many cases because the ink with which it has been signed is of a different color from the typing, whereas on the copy there will be just one color. All this is bound to make problems for the scholars of the future, and enhances the importance of identification of copies made in archival agencies by the name of the repository and the location of the original document.

Spurious Documents

On rare occasions researchers may be confronted by fraudulent or erroneously identified papers. However rare the cases, one should be aware of the possibility. There must be a motive for the forging of a document, and usually it is either to create an item that can be published at a profit or sold on the collector's market, or to effect a current action. The latter might be a real estate transaction, the submission of evidence in a lawsuit, or the influencing of voters in a political campaign. The historian may expect that the second class of forgeries would be discovered before the time comes for him to use the materials. But the creation of a document for sale is usually an effort to produce a "historic" item long after it was alleged to have been originated, and thus it may make its way into a group of historical sources.

An often-cited forgery made for sale and publication consisted of alleged correspondence of Abraham Lincoln and Ann Rutledge, which sold to a leading magazine for publication in 1928. After the letters had been accepted by several scholars and their publication had begun, it was realized from the erroneous references to the number of sections in a township (on which Lincoln would surely have been correct), a reference to Kansas several years before that name came into use, and several other errors, that they must be fraudulent.[5] The motive, to sell the letters for publication, seems more obvious in that case than in the fabrication of diaries, maps, court records, and physical objects on which was based part of a three-volume publication called *The Horn Papers: Early Westward Movement on the Monongahela and Upper Ohio, 1765–1795,* which appeared in 1945. A prodigious amount of work must have been done, perhaps only for glorification of a family name.[6] One of the most intriguing tales of fraud is that of supposed biographical materials relating to nonexistent persons. In *Appleton's Cyclopaedia of American Biography,* a well-known late nineteenth-century reference work, appear at least forty-seven sketches of individuals who were invented by writers eager to earn more in their space-rate compensation.[7]

At times, individuals simply do not recognize documents that are actually copies or artificial creations. This writer has received three letters in recent years from persons each of whom said that he had the "original" of the Declaration of Independence, one offering it for sale. They were no doubt well-intentioned citizens who had reproductions made for public sale many years ago which therefore looked old. During World War II an Allied intelligence officer drew up what he believed to be a statement of the German General Rommel's estimation of the situation in North Africa. The transmittal letter covering it was lost, and the document was widely published as a supposedly captured authentic German document.[8]

5. Paul Angle, "The Minor Collection: A Criticism," *Atlantic Monthly,* 143 (1929): 516–25; Allan Nevins, *The Gateway to History,* rev. ed. (Garden City, N.Y.: Doubleday, 1962), pp. 143–44.

6. "The Horn Papers," *Mississippi Valley Historical Review,* 34 (1947): 528–30; Arthur P. Middleton and Douglass Adair, "The Mystery of the Horn Papers," *William and Mary Quarterly,* 3d ser., 4 (1947): 409–45.

7. Nevins, *Gateway to History,* p. 151.

8. Air Force Manual 210–1, *Manual for Air Force Historians* (Washington: Department of the Air Force, 1952), pp. 7–8.

Internal Criticism

Analysis of the credibility of the statement, or internal criticism, though vital to historical research, is not as pertinent to our discussion here as external criticism. It is common to all kinds of historical evidence, rather than being predominantly a matter of analyzing primary sources. This kind of analysis should, however, begin while the researcher has the materials before him if he is working in an archival repository.

A researcher studying the relations of the United States and France between 1871 and 1914, for instance, might satisfy himself easily as to the authenticity of the dispatches sent back by the ministers and filed in the Department of State. But the value of the information contained will vary widely according to the competence of the men serving at that post, their prejudices in observing French leaders and events, their sense of duty in filing accurate reports, and other characteristics. These are matters that the scholar must work out from all the information that he can obtain about the men, the instructions under which they worked, the situation, and the comparison of dispatches of one period with those of another. This is all part of the work that the historian should expect to do for himself.

What the Researcher Does with the Facts

A more serious view of the scholar's use of sources than that in Mark Twain's advice to Rudyard Kipling is basic to the role of both the archivist and the user. Samuel Eliot Morison, in an address before the American Historical Association in 1950, made a strong case for the objective of the historian to "explain the event as it happened," quoting the German historian Leopold von Ranke. This entails, said Morison, an effort to present the truth with a high degree of intellectual honesty. To the archivist, this means that the scholar should use the sources as thoroughly as possible, and be open-minded in letting himself be guided by what they actually tell him, rather than simply choosing evidence to support his own prejudice. The archivist who spends great effort in preserving the documents and making them available to the historian, according to the highest standards that he knows, is bound to be disappointed if he feels that the user has wilfully chosen only the parts of the evidence that serve a predetermined purpose. This does not seem to be too idealistic an attitude for the archivist to take. After the historian has carried out his main objective of describing events "simply as they happened," as Morison urges, then it is his mission "to understand the motives and objects of individuals and groups . . . and to point out mistakes as well as achievements."[9]

9. Samuel E. Morison, "The Faith of a Historian," *American Historical Review,* 56 (1951): 261–75.

Changing Ways

The plethora of materials for the study of recent decades, and the technical processes that contribute to it, accentuate some research problems and inject new ones. At the same time, the new techniques have changed the use of older sources. The student should understand these developments, and though he will not be so directly involved in them as to need a technical manual, his comprehension of the newer modes is essential (even though the precepts of research that have been discussed hold for the study of any period of history). The repositories that have been mentioned, the nature of their holdings, their methods, and their finding aids, will change constantly. So will the fashions of historians in analyzing details or emphasizing broad phases of the human story.

"Papyrolatry"

Viewing the burgeoning of paperwork during World War II, the *Washington Post* suggested in 1942 that this might be known as the "age of papers," and that its preoccupation with forms and reports might be called "papyrolatry."[1] It seems to be characteristic of human beings, in personal life and especially in business and government, that more and more written documents are constantly being created and filed. Examples are all about us. The causes for this acceleration are many. There are more people in the world whose actions

1. Editorial, "Age of Papers," *Washington Post,* May 16, 1942.

must be recorded and who choose to express themselves in writing. There has been a concatenation of world wars, economic booms and crashes, political upheavals, and accelerated scientific developments. Governments and business organizations grow larger and more mechanized. The increased role of government in everyday society means that information about individual citizens is recorded to a greatly increased extent. Whether engaged in scientific tabulations, sociological analyses, medical studies, or political polls, research bodies constantly collect more and more data about all of us.

Mechanical means of creating records have contributed markedly to the increase of paperwork ever since 1874, the generally accepted date of the invention of the typewriter. Their development can be traced into bound books, and their filing in folders and cabinets. The problem of bulk in accumulated files already existed in 1904 when Claude H. Van Tyne and Waldo G. Leland prepared the first guide to federal government archives. They noted:

> The mere mass of these records of the government is well-nigh appalling. It is impossible to form an estimate of the aggregate space occupied by them. . . . In some departments entire buildings are rented for no other purpose than that of filling them from cellar to attic with records and files that are not in immediate demand in the prosecution of current work. Finally the widely varying value of the different classes of records constitutes a problem in itself. From the papers of the Continental Congress or the journals of the Confederate Congress to the correspondence relating to the pay or dismissal of a janitor there is a considerable depreciation in value.[2]

Technical changes accentuated the problems even further, through a series of changes in recordkeeping.[3] Following trends

2. Claude H. Van Tyne and Waldo G. Leland, *Guide to the Archives of the Government of the United States at Washington,* 2d ed. (Washington: Carnegie Institution of Washington, 1907), p. vi.

3. Harold T. Pinkett, "Investigations of Federal Recordkeeping, 1887–1906," *American Archivist,* 21 (1958): 163–92.

in private industry, a commission reporting to President Taft on office work in the government recommended the replacement of letter-press copybooks by carbon copies, and encouraged the use of subject file schemes.[4] While these recommendations were designed to economize personnel time, they also increased the proliferation of duplicate copies that caused the files to bulge.

Recent years have made duplication of papers easier than before, by photographic processes, offset printing, and the more sophisticated innovations of the broad and bewildering world of automation. Like the recommendations of the Taft Commission, these developments have been introduced primarily to speed current office processes, but they have also had the effect of causing files to grow and grow.

Mass and the Researcher

The mass of materials complicates the task of the researcher; it magnifies the intriguing challenge of finding, analyzing, and evaluating the sources. The user should understand some of the ways in which the trend affects the characteristics of his working materials, and he should at least be conscious of the current practices in handling records and the technical processes involved, even though he does not need to master them.

There are vastly greater quantities of sources relating to one person, organization, or topic now than one would find pertaining to a comparable subject of fifty years ago, and their nature is far more diverse. The researcher is confronted by all manner of typed documents, carbon copies, mimeographed or offset printed issuances that are still not published matter, punched cards, and the printouts of data-processing machines. Even the long dependable distinction between written and printed materials is growing less clear with the rapid growth of photo-offset and other facsimile processes.

4. Bess Glenn, "The Taft Commission and the Government's Record Practices," *American Archivist*, 21 (1958): 277–303.

Likewise, the complexity of filing has burgeoned. One example may be cited—not to imply that the Department of State is by any means the chief sinner, but because a pleasing contrast is provided by an early memorandum. Sometime in the early 1790's Henry Remsen, Jr., chief clerk in the department, wrote a memorandum in which he noted that the foreign letters which had not been filed away were kept in appropriate pigeon holes and drawers of his desk according to their kind, and then said:

> The letters from our Ministers, Chargé des affaires & Consuls will be sent to the Office to be filed from time to time by Mr. Jefferson; who will direct which shall be recorded. Observe the present mode of filing them. His foreign letters will be recorded in the foreign letter book— and his domestic letters in the domestic letter book, as before, and at the close of every year. Material papers enclosed and referred to in letters he writes, to follow the letter in the record.[5]

Throughout the nineteenth century, instructions and dispatches, and notes to and from foreign governments, were neatly organized in those series and bound in books. At the same time, the practice of copying them into bound blank books fell away. In 1906 the complexity of foreign affairs brought a numerical filing scheme that largely upset the old series. That lasted until 1910 when a classified subject-decimal file was adopted. It was amended and warped to the point that one can now find in it such a symbol as "763.72119/256," which designates a document relating to the termination of World War I, referring to its beginning over a dispute between Austria and Serbia. This example need not cause the researcher dismay; State Department and National Archives staffs know how to use the system, and a new subject-numeric filing scheme has been adopted in the department. But it illustrates what

5. Henry Remsen, Jr., "Mr. Remsen's Memo of the Disposition of Papers in the Department of State," Reports of Bureau Officers, vol. IA, 1790–1834, Record Group 59, National Archives.

has happened in all kinds of large organizations. In business and in private institutions, as well as in all levels of government, vast systems of records creation, receipt, registration, and filing of papers have proved necessary to get the day's work done.

Records Management

The accumulation of files is not wholly uncontrolled. Since early in World War II, a new activity has grown up within these large organizations, known as records management. Specialists in the handling of records, more concentrated than authorities in office management in general, have devoted themselves to the early life history of records, including "birth control," current routing and use, filing, storage, and disposition (in its broad sense.)[6] Their primary job is to make paperwork more effective for the creating offices. One major objective, both for this purpose and to serve posterity, is to improve the documentation of operation at policy levels. Preventing the creation of useless records, careful handling of papers in current use, and wise selection for retention are basic to the needs of the researcher. He cannot obtain a full and orderly body of evidence unless care is taken at the time it is filed, and he cannot understand the processes of the organization he is studying unless he knows something of its methods of documentation. Records management can improve the quality of the sources for the future scholar if it is carried out with a constructive interest in good documentation as well as a desire to economize. Archivists have done more than any other group to create the concept of effective records management, and they have a continuing concern in it. They are in turn working for the long-run benefit of the scholar.[7]

6. The present writer introduced the concept of the life history of records to emphasize the common interests of archivists and records managers: Philip C. Brooks, "The Selection of Records for Preservation," *American Archivist,* 3 (1940): 221–34.

7. Frank B. Evans, "Archivists and Records Managers: Variations on

What Records Are Saved?

The record of an event is usually not complete when the researcher sets out to study it. Not only are some things never recorded, but some documents once created are not kept. In his quest for all the information he can find, the student may be concerned both about accidental losses and about the fact that some papers are intentionally destroyed. Fires, floods, moves, and many other causes—including simple carelessness—have deprived researchers of many sources they would like to have available, as have the belief of persons in charge of records that they have no future value, or just their desire to clean house. The contrast between the considerable quantity of material on the early life of President Franklin D. Roosevelt and the paucity relating to President Truman's boyhood illustrates how families vary in this matter.

So far we have been discussing primarily factors that bring about the accumulation of overwhelming volumes of papers. It is axiomatic that if only that trend prevailed, we would all soon be buried under a layer of papers so thick that we would not be able to measure it. A concomitant of the accelerated growth of documentation has been the increased need for conscious elimination of some of it.

In the case of private papers, this process of disposal is usually quite informal. An individual may simply decide that papers he has kept take up too much space and cannot see that they might have future value for a student. His heirs often take the same view, especially when they must liquidate an estate on short notice. This is frequently true even though the individual, and, later his family, know that his activities have been important. Historical societies and other collectors of papers do a great service to scholarship by making such

a Theme," *American Archivists,* 30 (1967): 45–58. For a guide to the extensive literature of records management, both within and outside the government, see National Archives and Records Service, Office of Records Management, *Records Management Handbook: Bibliography for Records Managers* (Washington: National Archives and Records Service, 1964).

persons aware of the potential value of their materials. When that is done they may take the normally desirable action of discarding items that are clearly of only transitory value and at the same time save the correspondence and other papers that do have lasting interest—though admittedly their judgment as to enduring value cannot always prove correct in the long run.

The process of elimination becomes somewhat less informal as one moves to consider organizations of all kinds and families that are important for several generations. The most natural thing is still for people to throw out papers to save space. Even a local unit of government, though its officials may be conscious of their obligation to keep records of legal importance, is likely to be prompted mainly by space and equipment needs in deciding on disposition. The historian's need is apt to be considered only if some person in a church, club, union, or company is aware of the possible historical significance of its general files, including policy correspondence, photographs, and maps. One of the great problems is that even historically minded people usually think only of older materials as of value, and much of importance is lost for lack of a sense of value at the time when current office needs normally cause elimination of old files. It is in connection with these families, organizations, and local governments that researchers are most indebted to historical societies and others who seek to preserve historically significant records—to save the wheat and let the chaff go.

With larger organizations, such as county or even state governments, regional or national church bodies, labor unions, universities and colleges, and business firms, the practices vary widely. Many of them have well-ordered records programs which include the removal of unneeded files from working offices, their storage if necessary, careful analysis and evaluation, and eventual disposition by transfer to an archival agency or by elimination. One fortunate trend is the increased use of disposition schedules by which designated categories of records are evaluated in advance and removed from files or storage at stated intervals. Thus their evaluation does not have to await the time when they have accumulated to an excessive volume, or when they have become "historical" in the sense of being old.

Large organizations are often found to have their own archives for preservation of records of lasting value. Examples are too numerous to warrant the citing of a few, but some are referred to in chapter 2, and many articles have appeared about them in the professional journal, *American Archivist*.

Because it was creating great volumes of records, the federal government was obliged to initiate large-scale planned disposal programs soon after the establishment of the National Archives. They culminated in disposal legislation approved in 1943. Soon after that, a subsequent act authorized the use of disposition schedules.[8] The expediting of disposition was essential because of the wartime flood of records, which also brought about the beginning of records management programs. At the same time, the military services established records centers, which later became parts of the National Archives and Records Service of the General Services Administration.

The difficult task of evaluation requires an understanding both of the immediate usefulness of records and their potential research value. The development of principles and guidelines has been painstaking and slow. It has inevitably brought some differences of opinion for which there are no ideal solutions except good judgment. For example, most records managers and some archivists feel that chronological files of outgoing correspondence (often known as "day" or "reading" files) do not warrant preservation. Yet many archivists, including this writer, know that such files for important offices are often useful to the researcher. This is clearly a matter that must be decided on the basis of the significance of what is normally done in individual offices or classes of offices. The establishment of evaluation standards for individuals and smaller organiza-

8. 57 Stat. 380, July 7, 1943; 59 Stat. 434, July 6, 1945. The need for a clear definition of "records" to be covered by the act of 1943 led to wording that has been widely adopted at all levels of government and to some extent in nongovernment organizations.

tions is difficult because appraisal may depend on particular circumstances, but general guidelines are possible. The best ones are knowledge of the general needs of historians, and common sense.[9]

In the federal government the emphasis is on evaluation, so that identification and preservation of useful materials are at the core of the process. Vast quantities must be removed from working files by transfer to archival custody or by elimination. This is done as much as possible by the creating agencies, in accordance with schedules drawn up in concurrence with the National Archives. The interests of researchers are explicitly stated in the disposal law of 1943, which uses the phrase "administrative, legal, and historical value."

Duplication of Sources

Once the content of groups of sources in repositories has been determined, their availability to users can be greatly enhanced by processes of duplication. The problems of modern mass have forced the adoption of significant innovations in this field, and they in turn have facilitated the use of older sources. The use of duplication processes by individual scholars has been discussed in chapter 5; we are now considering the duplication of whole groups of papers for several purposes.

Some records, usually those that must be retained for administrative or legal use but are rarely used, are duplicated for economy of space and the originals destroyed. Records that are indispensable for operating purposes are often microfilmed for security. We are more concerned with a third use of duplication of whole groups, which is to make sources more available to students.

9. Appraisal standards are discussed in T. R. Schellenberg, *Modern Archives,* pp. 133–60. Many articles on evaluation in various fields have been published in the *American Archivist* through the years. Federal government regulations affecting the public are stated in the *Guide to Record Retention Requirements,* of which the latest annual issue is in the *Federal Register,* 33 (1968): 4002–79.

Early examples of this last type of activity were the copying of records pertaining to American history in European archives. Representatives of many institutions traveled abroad making copies by arduous longhand transcription. The practice grew substantially with the introduction of photographic processes; first by full-sized facsimiles, which were more accurate, more quickly made, and cheaper; and then by microfilm, still quicker and less expensive. Notable examples of this have been the vast project of the Library of Congress known as "Project A," and the activities of several universities.

The introduction of photographic processes also made possible on an enlarged scale the duplication of sources within the United States. Examples of this are legion, one of the largest being conducted both here and abroad by the Church of Latter-Day Saints to copy genealogical records.[10]

Most of the duplication of sources has been on microfilm. Despite its inconveniences and the need for reading equipment, it is more practicable and widely adopted than microduplication on cards, and other variations. These will undoubtedly be further developed and it behooves the scholar to be alert to progress in this as in related technical fields.[11] (In any form, microcopies of documentary sources are not treated here as a special physical type of materials, because they are reproductions of texts and used in the same way for study.)

Duplication of sources is one solution for the dispersal of papers and the overlapping of holdings of repositories mentioned in chapter 2. Archivists normally seek papers in the subject or regional fields of their institutions. Sometimes they acquire papers that one might expect to find elsewhere in order

[10] Archibald F. Bennett, "The Microfilming Activities of the Genealogical Society of the Church of Jesus Christ of Latter Day Saints," *Archivum*, 9 (1959): 121–23.

11. Policies and problems of repositories regarding duplication of sources are discussed in Walter F. Rundell, Jr., "To Serve Scholarship," *American Archivist*, 30 (1967): 547–55. Microfilm holdings of repositories as of 1961 are listed in Richard W. Hale, Jr., comp., *Guide to Photocopied Historical Materials in the United States and Canada* (Ithaca: Cornell University Press, 1961).

to prevent the loss of valuable sources that would otherwise be destroyed. They often take papers because the donors choose to place them in certain localities or certain institutions. This latter factor, the wish of the donors, is generally overlooked by researchers, but is a real one for the archivist. It is more responsible than anything else for the occasional dispersal of the papers of one individual in two or more repositories. These cases are particularly appropriate for microfilm duplication and exchange among repositories. Such exchanges have already taken place among private institutions and the presidential libraries, and fortunately the reluctance of some institutions to duplicate their holdings is lessening.

Microfilm Publication

A refinement of the duplication process has come in recent years in microfilm publication. The National Archives has microfilmed important series with some supplementary editorial matter analogous to that of a published series of documents in letterpress. This program began with the diplomatic correspondence up to 1906, and many other series are being added. The film is sold to institutions and individual scholars to pay the cost of editing and filming. The Library of Congress has published on film most of the bodies of presidential papers that are in its Manuscript Division, and its program is continuing. Among many other projects is the microfilming of the papers of the Adams family by the Massachusetts Historical Society.

More recently, a number of other repositories have microfilmed bodies of papers, many of them under the aegis of the National Historical Publications Commission. For the most part these are papers that are valuable for research but that do not warrant the expense of letterpress publication. The variety of these projects is seen in the filming of the records of Spanish and Mexican administration of New Mexico, 1688–1846, by the New Mexico Records Center and Archives; the records of Dakota Territory, 1861–89, by the University of North Dakota; the papers of Thomas Penn by the Historical Society of Pennsylvania; and those of Warren G. Harding by the Ohio Historical Society.[12]

Oral History

One ancillary development that warrants mention here because of its close relationship to the preservation of archives and private papers, and because its products are usually kept among them, is oral history. Archival institutions are among the agencies that have taken part in this effort to supplement the written record by the creation of new unpublished sources. Oral history began at Columbia University in 1948 under the leadership of Professor Allan Nevins. Interviewers using tape recorders question participants in historic events or periods. They seek accounts of actions that were never recorded, explanations of motives that do not appear on paper, and other elusive elements of history.

While historians have used interviews for centuries, oral history as it is now known has the additional result of creating sources that will be available to all interested scholars. For this reason the questioning should be carefully planned to cover a broader scope than the interests of any one researcher. The results are best when the interviewer has studied the subject field thoroughly, and especially when he has reviewed the papers of the person to be interviewed. Thus archival institutions seek papers both to add to their holdings and for use in oral history. The products of oral history are for the most part typed transcripts that are filed with other unpublished

12. National Archives, *List of National Archives Microfilm Publications, 1966* (Washington: National Archives and Records Service, 1966); Fred Shelley, "The Presidential Papers Program of the Library of Congress," *American Archivist,* 25 (1962): 429–33; Lyman H. Butterfield, "Vita sine literis, mors est; the Microfilm Edition of the Adams Papers," *Library of Congress Quarterly Journal of Accessions,* 18 (1961): 53–58; Frank B. Evans, "American Personal Papers," *Library of Congress Quarterly Journal of Accessions,* 22 (1967): 147–51.

sources. Some institutions save the tapes as well, but practically all have the transcripts typed, and then reviewed by the persons who have been interviewed.

Oral history depends upon memory, often of persons of advanced age. Its products must thus be subject to especially careful criticism by the user. The saving grace of the process is that the interviewer who prepares himself by background study can prod the memory of the respondent. He can even question statements of fact or interpretation during the discussion, though after the questioning he must leave the interviewee free to his own explanations, interpretations, and opinions. This informed interviewing is intended to remove from oral history products some of the skepticism that historians properly have of the words of forgetful people.[13]

Automation and Historical Research

The new and puzzling realm of electronic data-processing seems far from the traditional use of the letters of our forebears. Yet it is bound materially to affect the world of the historian. This is not the place for even a beginning essay on automation, but the scholar needs to know how it may change the course of his work. Electronic "brains" do not really think, but they perform repetitive tasks at unbelievable speed; they make possible the finding of information by immediate selection rather than by running through an entire film or file of papers; and they can store information for future use, arrange it, compile data, and "print out" results. These capabilities are being used in the service of scholarship in several ways. One of the problems in understanding them is that a new and rapidly changing vocabulary is growing, as in any new scientific field, and laymen

13. The value of oral history products to researchers was among the topics discussed at the first two oral history colloquiums: *Oral History at Arrowhead: The Proceedings of the First National Colloquium on Oral History . . . 1966* (Los Angeles: Oral History Association, 1967), and *The Second National Colloquium on Oral History . . . 1967* (New York: Oral History Association, Inc., 1968).

may easily be confused.[14] (An example in a different field
was a graduate student in physics who was especially pleased
to be invited to present a paper at a national meeting because
one scientist was to attend who would be the only person who
could understand the paper aside from the graduate student
himself and his own professor.)

Data-processing techniques will be encountered by the historian in three general manifestations: the preparation of improved finding media for existing types of sources; the use
of new techniques for compiling data from or evaluating existing
sources; and the creation of entirely new forms of records, if
they can be called that, from current processes. The last is the
least understood by researchers and the most unpredictable.

One of the first adaptations of automation to finding information among sources, a form of the widely discussed field of
information retrieval, was the preparation of indexes by the
use of punched cards. At the Library of Congress, to cite one
of the first and largest applications, indexing of names is being
done by this method in connection with the project for microfilming the presidential papers. The Public Archives of Canada
likewise provides subject indexing of names for an extensive
project involving the contents of papers of the prime ministers.[15]

Many collections, however, are too large to index, or facilities
do not exist in the repositories to prepare item indexes. In this
situation the Manuscript Division of the Library of Congress
again took the lead. From existing catalogs and other finding
aids, a master record was prepared on punched cards, thus
bringing together the descriptive information available regard-

14. A useful statement of elementary terms for the layman is Ralph
W. Parker, "What Every Librarian Should Know about Automation,"
Wilson Library Bulletin, 38 (1964): 752–54. A valuable guide is Bar-
bara Fisher and Frank B. Evans, "Automation, Information, and the
Administration of Archives and Manuscript Collections: Bibliographic
Review," *American Archivist,* 30 (1967): 333–48.

15. Russell M. Smith, "Item Indexing by Automated Processes,"
American Archivist, 30 (1967): 295–302; Jay Atherton, "Mechaniza-
tion of the Manuscript Catalogue at the Public Archives of Canada,"
ibid., 303–9.

ing the 3,000 collections in the division. This program, like the National Union Catalog of Manuscript Collections, has had the salutary effect of bringing forth improved finding aids. It has led to the recording of 98 separate items of information about each collection, including title, date, size, location, restrictions, provenance, and NUCMC card numbers. Most of these can now be retrieved in computer-printed lists which aid prospective users of collections. A punch card call slip enables the user to enter his request on a form that is actually part of the automated system.[16]

The National Archives is developing a program for using data-processing techniques to improve and gather together its own finding aids to the hundreds of record groups in the institution, somewhat similar to the plan of the Library of Congress mentioned above. It is also coordinating a program to produce finding aids by automated methods among ten institutions; this program is known as SPINDEX II. The aims of this program have been described as indexing finding aids, providing interinstitutional indexing, re-creating finding aids, producing new finding aids from box lists, updating finding aids, retrieving information in other than its original format, and developing a generalized indexing program. The possibilities of assistance to the scholar, who is the intended chief beneficiary of this planning, are immense.

Historical Analysis by Quantification

The techniques that researchers in many fields have had to develop for handling the masses of records of recent decades, and the growth of automated processes, have brought new emphasis to the study of history by quantification. Historians have long given attention to measurable phenomena and to statistical analysis, but mid-twentieth-century trends have brought

16. Frank G. Burke, "The Application of Automated Techniques in the Management and Control of Source Materials," *American Archivist,* 30 (1967): 255–78.

far greater use of these methods—and extensive debate over their effectiveness. In large measure because the machines make possible computations far more complex and far more rapid than before, historians are now able to approach familiar problems from new bases of inquiry.

Quantitative studies of demographic characteristics, popular and legislative voting patterns, economic circumstances, and group characteristics offer opportunities for analysis by data-processing techniques. It may seem strange to say that the American colonial period has been more extensively analyzed by these methods than recent decades, but the historians studying eighteenth-century America have been pathfinders in this kind of research.[17] What would our colonial ancestors have thought if they had been told they were to be studied by computers?

Professor Samuel P. Hays has emphasized the value of data processing for the study of the social background of economic and political history, and has noted that quantitative analysis can stimulate interest in local history and in genealogy. Through the Inter-university Consortium for Political Research, centered at the University of Michigan, and with the sponsorship of the Social Science Research Council and the American Historical Association, much has been done by political scientists, historians, and archivists to gather basic quantitative data of American political history.[18] Much of the local government data are to be found still in the administrative agencies, or reproduced in newspapers, rather than in archival agencies.

Possibilities of study by data-processing methods are wide, though they depend upon the availability of information that can be expressed in measurable terms. Some historians feel that the emphasis on group characteristics overlooks the appreciation of personal qualities of individuals, leaders, and citizens. They might say that computers will take much of the

17. Samuel P. Hays, "Archival Sources for American Political History," *American Archivist,* 28 (1965): 17–30.
18. Jerome M. Clubb and Howard Allen, "Computers and Historical Studies," *Journal of American History,* 54 (1967): 599–607.

fun out of history. It does seem difficult to express in measurable terms the reasons why things were done by persons in authority, explanations of individual reactions, changes in the states of mind of leaders, the problems weighed in decision-making, or the color that comes with the personal touch.

But those who use computer techniques in the study of archives know all this. A keen evaluation of these methods has been presented by Professor William O. Aydelotte:

> Quantitative procedures by no means preclude, nor indeed can they possibly eliminate, the use of value judgments, speculations, intelligent guesses, or "the imagination and intuitive feel which the historian, and for that matter the social scientist, should bring to his subject." What is gained . . . is not the elimination of subjective factors but the minimizing of their role. . . . I am disturbed by students who want to do quantitative research and who seem to expect that this will solve their problems and that the application of a method will save them the trouble of thinking.[19]

Professor Hays expressed a wish for doctoral and postdoctoral training of historians when he stressed that they should learn data location and development, data manipulation, sampling, and research design.[20] Once he has a specific problem, the researcher can use a knowledge of these processes to determine whether or not quantification studies are appropriate to its solution.

The collections of data accumulated at such a research center as that at the University of Michigan, and used in research

19. William O. Aydelotte, "Quantification in History," *American Historical Review,* 71 (1966): 803–25. A forceful statement of the ineffectiveness of quantitative analysis for the study of many kinds of problems is given in Arthur M. Schlesinger, Jr., "The Humanist Looks at Empirical Social Research," *American Sociological Review,* 27 (1962): 768–71.

20. Hays, "Quantification in History: The Implications and Challenges for Graduate Training," *American Historical Association Newsletter,* vol. 4, no. 5 (1966): 8–11.

by data processing, are sometimes referred to as "archives"—
which they are not. They were not produced in the current
processes of the activity being studied, and they have lost much
of their character as evidence. They are, rather, collections
of source data drawn from primary sources. This distinction is
significant when we are confronted by the third aspect of the
scholar's interest in automation. That is the creation of records
in current processes that produce machine-readable products
which are not documents in the familiar sense at all.

Automation in Current Processes

A substantial share of the business of governments and business firms, and perhaps to a lesser extent of other private institutions and organizations, is conducted in measurable terms.
Their current activities can be and are being conducted by
the use of automatic data-processing machines. The products
cannot be read by use of the human eye and the alphabet,
but require newly developed scientific techniques.

These current processes use electronic devices for the manipulation of data, and the products are for the most part punch
cards and magnetic tapes. At first, those were thought of as
intermediate working materials, not having lasting quality as
archives, a characteristic that would adhere only to the "input
and output" records. But, especially in the federal government
because of the vastness of its operations, it became evident
that agencies were relying on the machine products as having
long-time archival value.

In basic principles, these records constitute another special
type, which archivists and scholars face as they did cartographic
materials, still photographs, and moving pictures long ago.
All of them must be appraised for their informational value,
and ways must be developed to preserve them, to make their
contents known, and to make them available for users. The
products of automation present much more specialized problems, however. Their permanence is yet undetermined, they are
difficult to handle without damage, and they cannot be "read"

without the use of expensive, complex, and rapidly changing machines.[21] Anyone who has bought a tape recorder and used it a few years knows the problems of repair and obsolescence on a comparatively Lilliputian scale.

Archivists have special problems in establishing the integrity of their automated holdings which they must solve in order to be able to explain them to eventual scholars. Dr. James B. Rhoads, the Archivist of the United States, said recently:

> Data on a "master tape" may come from many sources, physically reflect very poorly the "original arrangement" as it relates to actual transactions, and it may be changed, added to or re-sorted, depending on which key, or "program," is used to unlock the data from the tape. Print-outs tend to freeze the data in only one of their facets or modes and thereby lose much of the evidential character of the data. I am not raising these issues as unsolvable problems. They are by no means unsolvable nor have the basic principles been abrogated. If the archivist can master the complexities of modern paper recordkeeping systems, he can make machine language respond to principle.[22]

The kinds of materials that are being accessioned by the National Archives as of lasting value are, to cite its first example, 38,000 reels of magnetic tape of the Bureau of the Census for the period 1954–59. The "documentation," constituting explanatory material for use of the tapes, accompanied them. Other examples have been magnetic tapes resulting from the Consumer Price Index and the Consumer Expenditure Survey, from the Bureau of Labor Statistics (for which the explanatory

21. The archival problems were well and briefly stated for a round table of the International Council on Archives in Morris Rieger, "Archives and Automation," *American Archivist,* 29 (1966): 109–11. See also, bibliographical citations in Fisher and Evans, "Automation, Information, and Archives."

22. James B. Rhoads, "Archival Values of Machine-Readable Data," paper read at a symposium on "Automation: Its Effects on Archives and Research in History and the Social Sciences," Atlanta, Ga., March 14, 1968, p. 5.

"documentation" is on punched cards); and magnetic tapes from the Economic Research Service of the Department of Agriculture. Almost 35 per cent of the records of the National Aeronautics and Space Administration are reported to consist of magnetic tapes, and some are being transferred to the National Archives.

Whether or not researchers can use these tapes effectively depends upon the quality of the documentation that the creators of the tapes produce and preserve. The documentation consist of the programming that is developed, copies of "input documents" and codes that are used, information as to the controls of the output, memory allocation, equipment required, and other elements described in the sophisticated language of automation. The user may hope that this will all be assembled in a program manual or "run book."[23]

The implications of all this for the scholar are unpredictable, but the methods will be suggested by the research staffs of the producing agencies, for they must develop means of using these materials currently. The scholars who have used automation in analysis by quantification have already opened vistas for the future. What Archivist Rhoads said recently about the problems of the archivist applies as well to that of the researcher:

> . . . in the Federal Government, the substantive programs, such as disease prevention, safety programs, and even battle plans are being automated now. Our analysts estimate, to put the point a bit differently, that a very substantial portion of all correspondence and reporting could and should be mechanized. Certainly the bases for decisions are going to come more and more from data banks. Land records are rapidly being put on the computer. So are many records relating to our rights as citizens.

Dr. Rhoads went on to list several steps that had been taken toward solving the problems presented by machine language

23. Everett O. Alldredge, "Documenting ADP Operations," paper read at Interagency Records Administration Conference, Washington, D.C., September 16, 1966.

records, and to ask the cooperation of historians in this effort.[24]

The Wealth of the Indies

Research calls for individual resourcefulness in seeking out not only facts but nuances of meaning, shading of factors, personal motivations, and other phases of the human story that cannot be absolute or precise. The more understanding the researcher can bring to the sources, the better he can apply this resourcefulness. "A man must carry knowledge with him if he would bring home knowledge," as Dr. Johnson said.

This manual can best conclude with emphasis on the scholar's knowledge of what he wants, how to find the sources, and how to explain his needs to the archivist; and his ability to mine the sources once he has found them, to select the essential items for his needs, to evaluate their dependability, and to understand their meaning. These requisites apply to the use of automated tapes as well as to that of ancient documents. No body of papers, no cooperative archivist, no data-processing machine is going to do the scholar's work or his thinking for him. But they can enable him to experience the excitement of finding information or formulating conclusions that are new to him and perhaps to the world in general. In the seminar of the late Professor Herbert E. Bolton, of California, a graduate student once read an especially revealing paper. When the reading had ended Professor Bolton said enthusiastically, "Now, you've told us something that nobody ever knew before!"

This writer believes that historical study is more than an exercise of the mind, as some scholars have insisted. It is a use of the mind for the purpose of achieving a better understanding of human civilization. And the cooperation of the researcher and the archivist to accomplish the most effective possible use of the sources has a significant part in it.

24. Rhoads, "Archival Values," p. 8.

Who knows? Perhaps the researcher who has achieved thorough mastery of the sources and has learned how to get along with archivists may be the beneficiary of an augmented research program at Westernland University by occupying an Ascot Chair of Historical Studies.

Selected Bibliography

Works dealing directly with the use of unprinted source materials in historical research, and written for the user rather than for the archivist, are few. Those that also consider the developments of the last decade and the problems of modern mass number even less. These circumstances have led to the writing of this manual. The bibliography of items pertinent to this approach to the subject is therefore brief.

The following list includes some of the useful published items that the researcher might consult if he wishes to pursue further the topics that are dealt with in this manual. Examples of various kinds of archival publications, and other tools, are cited in the footnotes. Many more references are listed in the annual "Writings on Archives, Current Records, and Manuscripts," which with slightly varying titles and prepared by a succession of compilers has been published in the *American Archivist* since 1943. The cumulative bibliographies prepared for sources of archival instruction at the National Archives and at the American University by Frank B. Evans, and available at the libraries of those institutions, are exhaustive and helpful.

This manual, as stated in the Preface, is intended to discuss problems in the use of archives and private papers, rather than to be in any sense a bibliographical work.

General References

These items deal with matters that are discussed in the manual but cannot be related to any one chapter exclusively:

American Historical Association. "Report of the Ad Hoc Committee on Manuscripts," *Proceedings of the American Historical Association, 1950*. Washington: Government Printing Office, 1951.

Gottschalk, Louis. *Understanding History: A Primer of Historical Method*. New York: Alfred A. Knopf, 1960.

Gray, Wood *et al. Historian's Handbook: A Primer of Historical Method*. 2d ed. Boston: Houghton Mifflin Co., 1964.

Hockett, Homer C. *The Critical Method in Historical Research and Writing*. New York: Macmillan Co., 1960.

Johnson, Allen. *The Historian and Historical Evidence*. New York: Charles Scribner's Sons, 1926.

Kane, Lucile M. *A Guide to the Care and Administration of Manuscripts*. Madison: American Association for State and Local History, 1960.

Langlois, Charles Victor, and Seignobos, Charles. *Introduction to the Study of History*. New York: H. Holt and Co., 1898.

Posner, Ernst. *American State Archives*. Chicago: University of Chicago Press, 1964. (Especially valuable here for its "Selective Glossary of Terms," pp. 369–71; and its "Basic Bibliography . . ." pp. 377–86.)

Posner, Ernst. *Archives and the Public Interest*. Washington: Public Affairs Press, 1967.

Schellenberg, T. R. *Modern Archives: Principles and Techniques*. Chicago: University of Chicago Press, 1956.

Chapter 1. Archives and Private Papers

Born, Lester K. "Archives," *Encyclopaedia Britannica,* 1958 ed., 2:288–92.

Cappon, Lester J. "Historical Manuscripts as Archives: Some Definitions and Their Application," *American Archivist,* 19 (1956): 101–10.

Holmes, Oliver W. " 'Public Records'—Who Knows What They Are?" *American Archivist,* 23 (1960): 3–26.

Leavitt, Arthur H. "What Are Archives?" *American Archivist,* 24 (1961): 175–78.

Leland, Waldo G. *Archival Principles: Selections from the Writings of Waldo Gifford Leland,* National Archives, Staff Information Paper no. 20. Washington: National Archives, 1955.

Posner, Ernst. "Archives," *Collier's Encyclopedia,* 1962 ed. (New York: Crowell Collier Publishing Co.) 2:556–557.

2. Finding the Sources

Billington, Ray A. "Guides to American History Manuscript Collections in the United States," *Mississippi Valley Historical Review,* 38 (1951): 467–96

Hamer, Philip M. *A Guide to Archives and Manuscripts in the United States.* Compiled for the National Historical Publications Commission. New Haven: Yale University Press, 1961.

Library of Congress, comp. *National Union Catalog of Manuscript Collections. 1959–1962,* and *Index.* 3 vols. Ann Arbor, Mich.: J. W. Edwards; Hamden, Conn.: Shoe String Press, 1962–64. *1963–1966,* and *Index.* 3 vols. Washington, D.C.: Library of Congress, 1965–67.

Van Tyne, Claude H., and Leland, Waldo G. *Guide to the Archives of the Government of the United States of America in Washington.* 2d ed. Washington, D.C.: Carnegie Institution, 1907.

3. The Researcher and the Archivist

Grover, Wayne C. "The National Archives and the Scholar," *Military Affairs,* 15 (1951): 5–10.

Jordan, Philip D. "The Scholar and the Archivist—a Partnership," *American Archivist,* 31 (1968): 57–65.

Lamb, W. Kaye. "The Archivist and the Historian," *American Historical Review,* 68 (1963): 387–88.

Smith, Alice E. "The Society as a Research Center," *Wisconsin Magazine of History,* 32 (1949): 271–83.

4. *Limitations on Access and Use*

Bordin, Ruth B. and Warner, Robert L. *The Modern Manuscript Library.* New York: Scarecrow Press, 1966.

Connor, Seymour V. "The Problem of Literary Property in Archival Depositories," *American Archivist,* 21 (1958): 143–52.

Cross, Harold L. *The People's Right to Know: Legal Access to Public Records and Proceedings.* New York: Columbia University Press, 1953.

Land, Robert H. "Defense of Archives against Human Foes," with comments by Lucile M. Kane and Richard D. Higgins. *American Archivist,* 19 (1956): 121–38.

Peckham, Howard H. "Policies Regarding the Use of Manuscripts," *Library Trends,* 5 (1957): 361–68.

Rhoads, James B. "Alienation and Thieving: Archival Problems," *American Archivist,* 29 (1966): 197–208.

Wittenberg, Philip. *The Law of Literary Property.* Cleveland: World Publishing Co., 1957.

5. *Notes and Copies*

See Gottschalk, Gray, Hockett, and Langlois items cited under "General References," above.

6. *Criticism of Modern Unpublished Sources*

Bernheim, Ernst. *Lehrbuch der historischen Methode und der Geschichtsphilosophie.* 3d ed. Leipzig: Verlag von Duncher und Humblot, 1903.

Chatfield, Helen L. "The Dating of Documents," *American Archivist,* 24 (1961): 171–74.

Nevins, Allan. *The Gateway to History*. Rev. ed. Garden City, N.Y.: Doubleday, 1962.

7. *Changing Ways*

Aydelotte, William O. "Quantification in History," *American Historical Review,* 71 (1966): 803–25.

Burke, Frank G. "The Application of Automated Techniques in the Management and Control of Source Materials," *American Archivist,* 30 (1967): 255–78. (The entire April, 1967, issue of the *American Archivist* is devoted to automated techniques.)

Fisher, Barbara and Evans, Frank B., "Automation, Information, and the Administration of Archives and Manuscript Collections: Bibliographic Review," *American Archivist,* 30 (1967): 333–48.

Glenn, Bess. "The Taft Commission and the Government's Record Practices," *American Archivist,* 21 (1958): 277–303.

Hale, Richard W., Jr., comp. *Guide to Photocopied Historical Materials in the United States and Canada.* Ithaca: Cornell University Press, 1961.

National Archives and Records Service, Office of Records Management. *Records Management Handbook: Bibliography for Records Managers.* Washington, D.C.: National Archives and Records Service, 1964.

Oral History Association. *Oral History at Arrowhead: The Proceedings of the First National Colloquium on Oral History . . . 1966.* Los Angeles: Oral History Association, 1967; *The Second National Colloquium on Oral History . . . 1967.* New York: Oral History Association, Inc., 1968.

Rundell, Walter J., Jr. "To Serve Scholarship," *American Archivist,* 30 (1967): 547–55.

Index